Web of Hope

Lynette Heywood

Published by New Generation Publishing in 2019

Copyright © Lynette Heywood 2019

First Edition

The author asserts the moral right under the Copyright, Designs and Patents Act 1988 to be identified as the author of this work.

All Rights reserved. No part of this publication may be reproduced, stored in a retrieval system or transmitted, in any form or by any means without the prior consent of the author, nor be otherwise circulated in any form of binding or cover other than that in which it is published and without a similar condition being imposed on the subsequent purchaser.

www.newgeneration-publishing.com

This one is for Ebo ♡

I'm reminding you because I need to remind myself sometimes

You've got this

Don't let the fire burn low

Look after the little girl within

Never show your weaknesses

If every day is a battle, then fight it

When you think you're on that floor

Just remember a woman is naturally embodied with strength & her vigour is encapsulated within

Never forget how powerful you really are

Prologue

In the distance, I could see cars and buses on a parkway leading up to the city centre. If I looked hard enough, I could make out the lights of a football ground. Beyond that was the hustle and bustle of the city; the tall buildings looked misty in the distance. The heavy rain made my vision blurry.

The sky was almost black above me, and the rain was relentless. It wasn't unusual weather for Manchester, and it reflected the mood of the small crowd gathered in Southern Cemetery. The atmosphere was sombre, and I could sense revulsion, suspicion and agitation among the so-called mourners. Tears were scarce at this funeral.

Today a rapist, an animal who had made so many lives hell, was being buried.

His three sons carried their father on their strong shoulders. Robert and David, the two older sons, looked calm, while the youngest son, Richard, looked troubled in a way that was difficult to describe.

It didn't matter to me how anybody felt. After all, it was me who had killed him.

I grimaced as I watched the young men lower their father into his hole, clumsily knocking the coffin. I had an image of it breaking in two and him, Richard Ellis, leaping out of the box and exposing me as his killer. I shook my head as if to shake away the reverie and I came out of my trance. I'd spent my life being controlled by this vile man.

I'd grown up with Ella Parker, Bess Holland and Nessa Brown, but they'd never really accepted me. Under Richard's orders, I was to make their lives hell, particularly Ella's.

Then Ella's younger sister, Josie, was savagely attacked, raped and left for dead. Ella and her friends believed I was the monster who'd done it. I'd been manipulated by Richard Ellis for so long that he could easily put me in the frame. But I knew it was Richard who had carried out the vicious attack and I knew why.

It was their mother, Christine Parker, who he wanted to hurt. Years earlier, Richard had raped her, and Ella had been the result of that vicious attack. Christine had protected Ella from the truth, but Richard was obsessed with the family, taking every opportunity he could to torment them until I finally put an end to his life.

I often get flashbacks to that day. Ella and her friends wanted to exact revenge on me for the crime they thought I'd committed. They'd arranged to meet me in a seedy hotel in Manchester, where they planned to kill me. Like a fool, I'd believed they wanted me sexually, and my dick took over; I went to see what they had to offer. The smutty set up makes me hard even to this day.

I thought Nessa was about to suck my dick when I spotted the syringe in Bess's hand. The fear was almost a turn on; I was so fucking horny at the time, I almost welcomed death.

Then Richard walked in. I don't know how he knew we were there, but he did. He looked a mess. After that, everything happened so quickly; it's almost a blur. I remember the Bailey brothers, friends of the girls, entering the hotel room. There was a lot of confusion, and I was still naked on the bed.

I spotted the syringe on the floor, and everyone's fate suddenly lay with me.

The split-second decision had altered my life and the lives of those who were with me. I hadn't known at the time how much that decision would impact my life and change my path. I just knew it had to be him.

As quick as a flash, I'd picked up the empty syringe and ran towards the big mass of people. I lunged the syringe into the back of Richard's neck. He had died instantly.

I thought about the destruction and despair he had caused over two generations. I thought of the families who had been bonded together by his evil. He deserved to die.

Now I was standing here at his funeral, and only a handful of people knew the truth about his death.

The service came to an end, and people threw soil onto his coffin. I was conscious of the rain as it banged noisily on tin pots that lay on the graves of others. Some of them held wilting flowers, but most were empty.

It was time to go. I didn't want to be caught up in a funeral. I just wanted to make sure he'd gone down that hole.

I spun around to make my exit but bumped straight into his youngest son and namesake, Richard. I looked into his eyes; they were the same as his fathers. I shuddered, this lad was not good news.

'Peter Lawrence,' he said with hatred in his voice, 'don't think for a minute it's over. Don't fuckin' think I don't know exactly what went on. Most people here couldn't give a shit, but he was my dad and my mentor.'

I wasn't sure what to say, I just felt hot. I felt the spittle gather at the side of my mouth. I wiped it clumsily with the sleeve of my black jumper. Fuck it, fuck Richard Ellis, fuck his kid.

'Not here Lawrence,' he hissed. 'One day, but not here.'

I might have been having another episode where I imagined voices and entire conversations with people. I had them often, in my room, in the street, and now here, at Richard's funeral

I shook my head. He'd gone, I looked towards the small, sombre crowd, I couldn't see him. I looked towards the main road, the parkway that connected our large council estate with our huge city, but he was nowhere to be seen.

I needed to get away from here. I needed to get home and forget it…………………………….

Part One

Chapter 1

Christine Mellor: 1970s

I woke up in a daze and immediately put my hand between my legs where I could physically feel what had been done to me. My body started to shake as I recalled the events of the night before. I closed my eyes as dizziness hit me and I tried to piece things together. I needed to remember, I needed to get a grip, but my head was swimming. Who was he? And, where had he come from? I tried hard to remember step by step what had happened. The effect of the alcohol from the night before wasn't helping.

Madge had wanted me to go babysitting with her and Maureen. We'd sort of become friends recently. She was nice, but we were very different, she was a bit posher. She wasn't from our estate but often stayed at her aunt's.

She didn't really have much to say, and because she wasn't a permanent fixture, it was difficult to get to know her properly. But she was ok, I liked her, and I think she liked me, so it worked.

I lived on a huge council estate that had been created in the 1920s. It had been an overspill for people who lived in the slums and squalor of industrial Manchester. It had taken years for us to become a community, but once it became a community, the inhabitants seemed to lock swords and become one.

It was nice to bring Madge into the flock, and she was beginning to see who we were. She already had a boyfriend, Jon, who lived on the estate; he was probably one of the reasons why she was here so often. He was a bit older but not by much. He was a grafter, a builder, who got picked up every day at the huge roundabout that was laden with beautiful flowers in the summer. The other builders from the estate would pick him up in a big truck that would take him to wherever they were due to work that day. All of them would be dressed in scruffy jeans, vests and big woolly jumpers and ruined boots; they all worked hard and played hard.

I was glad she'd asked me to go with her as I had nothing else to do, and it meant a night of freedom with no adults.

We would listen to records and talk about boys; I was nearly sixteen years old, and boys were starting to notice me. I had a trim figure and was starting to develop a nice curvy shape. I didn't like it much, but the boys certainly did, and I'd had a few asking me out.

We had called for Maureen Parker who lived up the road. Maureen and Madge had met through Maureen's older brother, Chris. He and Jon Holland had grown up together and often shared a few jars at the local pub.

Maureen and Chris had an older sister, Janet, and it was her flat that we would be babysitting at. Janet had a kid about two years old. No one knew who the dad was and nobody asked.

I lived near the woods next to a big field that was being turned into a motorway. There was nothing to separate you from the workmen but a brown wooden fence with black wiring. It was supposed to stop you entering the area, but instead, it helped with your footing if you ever had the inclination to climb it, which many people did. I'm sure they'd all stop once the cars started to flow. It was taking some getting used to the idea of a huge road taking the place of our lovely spacious greenery.

If you walked the opposite way from the woods along the newly made stone path, it would lead you to the new subway that looked like it would be part of the new road. Fluorescent lights reflected on our faces as our shadows jumped on the white walls that had already been covered in graffiti. I always had a feeling of dread walking through the subway. If I was on my own, I would run.

After walking through the subway, we'd turn right and walk up a black path that would lead us to a big blue bridge. It was unfinished, so we weren't supposed to use it, but we found a way. It was that or else we'd have to walk a mile to the next one to get to the other side.

Over the other side of the bridge was the same type of path we'd walked up but this time you had to walk down it. Next to it were hundreds of newly planted saplings that were starting to grow rapidly. They always gave me the creeps. The area was becoming a retreat for drunken men to keep shelter and drink their booze, and there had already been reports of attacks. I wasn't sure of the details and I didn't want to know either.

There was a big club at the end of the path where all the old Navy lads drank. Its wooden exterior was painted white, and there was a big anchor at the front that showed off the Union Jack proudly.

Not much further along, we arrived at five rows of flats that all looked the same. Maureen's sister, Janet, lived in the first block on the bottom floor.

The dark bushes that surrounded the flats almost made them look welcoming. There was a lot of greenery on the estate, a lot of trees and lots of grass; if you took the houses and flats away, it would feel like you were in the countryside.

When we arrived, Janet was all dressed up and ready to go out for the night. She was discreet about where she was going, but if truth be known, I didn't care. Janet had a reputation for sleeping with married men or anyone else that she could get; rumour had it she would sometimes take money for sex.

You'd never guess Janet got paid for anything going by the state of her flat. That said, she always looked the part and tonight was no different. She stood there in a sleeveless jumpsuit with a collar that sat high on her neck. Her brown wavy hair made her look like a TV star, and her trousers had the biggest flares you'd ever seen. Her perfume smelt like flowers.

I looked down at my own outfit and was suddenly very conscious of my scruffy flared jeans, scuffed white wedges and a black t-shirt which had white tubing around the sleeves and collar.

I couldn't wait for her to leave, but first, we had to go

through a drawn-out routine of complimenting her as she asked a hundred times how she looked. Because Madge was so quiet, and Maureen was her sister, it was down to me to reassure her.

'Yes, I love the red on you,' I said. 'No, definitely those shoes…. No, you don't need to get changed… You look great… Nope, those earrings are perfect…'

I was getting fucking bored now and was ready to say anything to get rid of her. Finally, she pulled out a fur coat. I didn't believe it was real; she wasn't earning that much. I feigned admiration for the coat; it looked like a dead squirrel.

'Do you want to try it on? Go on it'll suit you,' she said, holding it out to me. I had no choice but to try on a coat that I didn't want to try on, while the other two sat there saying nothing.

I just wish she would fuck off out now. I couldn't wait to look through her record collection and root through her drawers and wardrobes. I liked the idea of pretending it was my flat, something I couldn't wait for.

I looked around. My place would look better than this shithole. Everything was brown and shabby including a brown velvet three-piece suite with tassels on the arms. The carpet was brown and yellow and had the faint stench of piss seeping from it. There was a brown unit in the corner, oblong-shaped with thin black legs holding it up. An orange lamp made a cosy glow, but the cosy glow didn't cover the piss smell. When you lifted the lid of the unit, there was a record player with LPs stacked neatly in a compartment next to it. It was the only thing in the flat that appeared to have any order.

Last time we came, I had been impressed by her LP collection. She had a good variety, including a great collection of Motown, which all of us loved.

Janet gave Maureen instructions. There was milk in the fridge for baby Kevin if he woke up, which he rarely did.

'Are you sure I look ok Chrissie?' she asked again.

'Oh my god,' I smiled, 'yes, just go.'

I walked down the hall and let her out of the front door, shutting it firmly behind me. Finally, she was gone.

I turned around. There was no carpet anywhere else in the flat and the floors were freezing. If you walked up the hall there were two bedrooms; one had a double bed with a split mattress and a pile of covers on it. She also had a dark brown chest of drawers and a big brown walnut wardrobe in the corner which was full of dresses, jeans and coats. We'd be trying them on later.

The other room wasn't much better. This was the kid's room, and there was not much more than a cot and what looked like a big wooden coffee chest turned upside down and piled high with baby clothes and nappies.

There were a few toys thrown in a pile in the corner that had the faint smell of baby sick to it. There was a built-in wardrobe that consisted of a white panelled door with a rail behind it.

It dawned on me that any other parent wouldn't allow their kids to babysit here, but my mum only noticed me when I was in her face. Once out of her sight, it was as if I was forgotten. I'm sure Madge's aunt wouldn't be pleased about her being here but Madge wasn't perturbed by it, she was nonchalant in everything she did.

My thoughts of smelly sick were soon forgotten when Maureen informed us that Janet had a couple of bottles of Martini in the fridge. 'She nicked it from my mum,' she laughed, 'we've had it for years.'

A few drinks later and we were dancing in the living room to The Supremes. I laughed as I watched Madge clearly enjoying slumming it with us. She never looked the part, but it didn't matter, we were having fun.

Suddenly, there was a knock on the door.

That knock would probably alter my whole existence; if only I'd had a crystal ball....

Chapter 2

Richard Ellis

It was Friday night and I was bored. I was at a dance at St Peter's, the club that belonged to the local church of the same name.

The dance was full of young men and women. They would drink the illegal alcohol that they smuggled in and start fighting with each other. It was the same every week.

Most of the lads were here to find a girl to have their way with. Other lads came with their mates just for a scrap or to cause mayhem with any love rivals. Fucking idiots if you ask me.

I came here on my own. I was different compared to the other lads; I didn't need a gaggle of mates. To be honest, I'd never encountered anyone that met my high standards; they were always dickheads wanting a shag and sounding so immature about it.

When I showed up, I stopped a room. The lads were uncomfortable as they watched their girls squirm in their seats next to them. They were intrigued by my good looks, smart dress sense and unruffled appearance.

I enjoyed watching the girls. I enjoyed the way they accidentally brushed past me. I enjoyed the puppy dog eyes trying to get my attention. I enjoyed my own mysterious approach and how it made them cream their knickers.

I loved the power I had over them.

The shit they played in here was starting to get on my nerves; no taste, no class. I had to get out. I wondered where I'd go next. It was still early.

I wondered if that slag with a kid was in, she was always good for a leg-over. Fuck it; I was going for it, whether she liked it or not. I was twenty-two and worked fucking hard. I deserved good things, and I deserved a good wet pussy every now and again.

I approached the shithole she lived in. I could hear the

music blaring out and guessed immediately she wasn't in. The slag must have gone out for a fuck. There was someone there though, maybe it wouldn't be a wasted trip after all.

I let myself in the main doors, walked up the smelly, dirty hallway and stood in front of the door to her flat. I put my head just close enough so that I wasn't touching the wooden door. I was sure there was shit on the letterbox.

It sounded like there was a bunch of girls in there. I was sure one of my cousins, Madge, did the babysitting here. Could I be arsed going in? I wasn't sure I could cope with a gaggle of stupid fucking girls.

I felt a stir in my pants and was reminded that I could cope just fine.

I ran to the back of my car for more alcohol; I was already ahead of the game. I knocked and waited, listening to the nervous, drunken giggles coming from within.

Madge opened the door and hesitantly let me in. We didn't really know each other. I didn't bother with family; my mother was enough to deal with.

I passed pleasantries, well I had to be courteous I suppose. As I walked into the stinking living room, I knew I was right about the slag not being in. This was even better though as her kid sister was here with her mate. They were young and intimidated by me, overwhelmed, in awe.

It looked like they were half pissed already. I got myself a cup from the kitchen and poured us all a drink.

A couple more cups and the music resumed. I relaxed as the two young slags danced, trying to impress me with their bodies. At one point, I thought they were going to end up as one sordid sexual mess the way they rubbed their bodies up against each other, the way they touched each other, with their tongues resting on the sides of their mouths. It was like my own personal strip show without the stripping. Yet.

Chapter 3

Christine Mellor

As soon as he walked in, I felt a heat between my legs. He was the most handsome man I'd ever seen. He was older than us but probably only by a few years. He wasn't like the usual lads that lived around here; this was a man, a man with style.

'Who is he?' I asked Madge as he went to the kitchen to get a cup.

'He's my cousin, Richard,' she responded. 'He's a snob; he thinks we are all beneath him and he doesn't usually even bother with me. He's a bit of a loner, doesn't have any mates, and we think he has a wife shacked up in a big house in Wilmslow. My auntie says he's a dark horse.'

'He's a dishy dark horse,' I said grinning.

'That's what everybody says, but he's not good news,' she said seriously.

As the music ramped up so did the atmosphere. I was aware he was watching me, and I danced for him, pretending I didn't realise, pretending there was only him and me in the room. I knew he was looking at Maureen too; I needed him to look at me, only me. I stuck my tits out and shook my arse; I did moves that I didn't realise I was capable of, and all the while, I watched him, watching me.

The warm feeling between my legs was rising and making me feel thrilled. I'd never wanted anything so much. I wanted to open my legs and rub myself against him. I wouldn't have actually done such a thing, but the fantasy was nice.

The alcohol was taking over. I'd never felt this horny before, I felt soaking wet between my legs and could feel a hard throbbing that I'd never experienced. I needed to release myself.

I walked into the kitchen where the sound of the music became a distant beat, the cars outside passed loudly, and I could hear the usual row outside the chippy. I leant on the sink and stuck my hands down my knickers. I rubbed the parts that felt hot and sticky.

I looked up and saw him standing in the doorway watching me. I think he was smiling as he leant on the door frame.

'Carry on,' he said, 'don't let me stop you.'

That turned me on even more; my breasts were tingling in my tight t-shirt, and he spotted my erect nipples.

Without warning, he grabbed me roughly by the arm. 'Let's go,' he demanded.

The warm feeling subsided as he marched me to the bedroom with the double bed, chest of drawers and walnut wardrobe; Janet's bedroom.

I felt anxious. I didn't expect this. I don't know what I expected, but he was going too fast for me.

He pushed me roughly into the room and pulled my hair.

'That hurt,' I said, trying to make him realise that I wasn't comfortable with what he was doing. He forced his face onto mine and started sucking on my lips in a way that made me feel repulsed. He pulled at my clothes.

A sense of panic came over me as his intensity grew and he ignored my protests. I wanted out.

Too late.

I was on my back on the ruffled bed that hadn't been made properly in years and stunk of piss. He was unfastening his pants, and he looked angry. I was worried he would hit me. My knickers were around my ankles.

I felt sick.

I tried to push him off. He wouldn't budge, he was heavy and he was strong.

I tried to squeeze my thighs together so he couldn't get inside me.

'Open them. You wanted this,' he said. He made me grab his rock-hard penis. 'Feel this. That's your fucking fault.'

I opened my legs slowly, hoping he'd realise I didn't want this and would back off.

He didn't.

I felt the hot, sharp thrust, followed by a stabbing feeling as he started to ride me, roughly forcing himself inside me as I tried with all my might to resist.

'Get off, please,' I begged.

He put his hand over my mouth and called me a cunt.

Finally, it was over. He got off me and slapped my face hard.

I was gobsmacked, totally and utterly gobsmacked. What the fuck had just happened?

I sat on the bed trying to get myself together as he pulled his pants up. I started to cry and he grabbed my face roughly.

'You wanted it,' he said, 'I watched you dancing with the other girl; you were gagging for it, you stuck your fingers up your pussy for me.'

I was too confused to respond; I was too scared to tell him to get off.

'Stop crying now,' he said softly, but when I didn't stop, he shook me hard and threw me roughly back on the bed.

'You deserved it, you cunt,' he spat at me.

Then he left, leaving me in a daze.

I could hear the dulcet tones of Marvin Gaye's 'Let's get it on,' and I couldn't think of anything more inappropriate. That song would haunt me forever.

Chapter 4

Richard Ellis

Stupid slag. She led me on; standing with her hand down her knickers, her fucking nipples screaming at me. She was begging for it then wanted to change her mind. No fucking way. Did she think I would just walk away? Did she think I was fucking stupid?

What was it with these fucking girls?

I wiped myself down in the filthy bathroom and straightened myself up. It was time to get out of here. That fucking kid got what she deserved and what she wanted, dancing all night like she was a fucking whore, only I wasn't paying for it.

As I walked out of the vile smelling flat, I could see her down the hall. She was still sitting on the bed, probably regretting what she'd done. Too late; she'd done it.

She had been begging for it and I gave it to her. All the struggling was part of her act, but I loved the struggle, loved how weak she felt beneath me, loved how powerful it made me feel. It didn't repulse me at all; in fact, it turned me on so much that it was preventing my cock from going down in my pants as I left.

I got in my car and looked at myself in the mirror as I adjusted it. I put the radio on and Karen Carpenter harped on about how we'd only just begun. I laughed at the irony of the song. I'd only just begun with that little tease.

I could tell it was her first time. She was tight and fresh, not like the other slags I'd been fucking lately. I loved what she did to me, loved the way she squeezed her legs together tight so I couldn't get to her. But I did; she let me in eventually.

I drove to the unfinished bridge and sat in my car with the engine running, the adrenalin still pumping through my blood. I looked at the shite around me. I didn't know what I was doing here. I didn't have to be here. I had a good job as a police officer. I had authority and people respected me.

I sat for a while contemplating my next move.

Then I spotted her in my rear mirror.

She seemed so vulnerable, walking with the wind against her face, her black hair blowing to one side. She pushed hard against the wind, obviously still drunk, but not half as drunk as she'd been earlier.

I wanted her again.

I left the car and slowly made my way to the trees, being careful not to make any noise. I waited until I could hear her stomping up the path to the side of where I was hiding.

I didn't hesitate. I pounced, covering her mouth and dragging her to the ground. Then I gave her a second helping of what she'd got before.

Chapter 5

Christine Mellor

It wasn't long before I was awake again, the same dread hitting me hard in my stomach.

I pictured myself in the kitchen of that flat. What had come over me? Maybe it was the two bottles of alcohol I'd devoured earlier. I was wanton, and it had turned him on. He had wanted me, just as I'd hoped he would, but it had all turned sour, very sour.

The attack by the bridge was worse. I was still trying to make sense of what had just happened when he appeared from nowhere. It was like a nightmare that I couldn't wake up from.

I shook as I thought about him on top of me in the bushes with his hand firmly over my mouth. I'd tried to bite him, struggled hard, but it was to no avail. He'd already taken my virginity in the most violent way, but it wasn't enough for him.

I needed a bath. I could smell him, I could smell the piss and sick of the flat, I could smell the leaves of the bushes. I needed to wash it all off.

I discreetly made my way to the bathroom before anyone in our house could see me. The last thing I wanted to do was cause a fuss, my mum would fucking kill me, and my dad would kill him.

After washing myself thoroughly but not feeling any cleaner, I made my way to where Madge was staying with her aunt.

Most of the estate is made up of rows and rows of the same terraced houses, but this part of the estate is unique. It's a close, not an avenue or a road, a close. It has maisonettes that form a square with grass in the middle.

Even though it was broad daylight and the birds were chirping brightly from the woods that grew wildly at the back of the close, I was paranoid as I walked. I felt on edge, imagining him hiding in the trees, watching and waiting for me as he had done last night.

I reached Madge's, hoping and praying she was in. I walked up the path which had a big tiled step at the end leading up to the front door.

I knocked and waited. I was grateful when it was Madge herself that answered the door, but she didn't look pleased to see me. My stomach turned.

'Erm, I'm not coming out,' she said. She looked back down the hall. 'He's here,' she whispered, 'I'll call for you later.'

I ran. I didn't look back; the idea of seeing him filled me with dread.

I wasn't sure where to turn next. The air was stale, or maybe I was imagining it. I didn't know; the confusion I was feeling right now was superseding any reality.

I found myself walking over to Janet's flat to see if Maureen was there. I'm not sure why.

Janet wasn't in when I arrived, nor was Maureen. The door was answered by their brother Chris. I stood and stared at him, my knees trembling. I burst into tears and the poor lad didn't know what to make of it. He put his arm gently around my shoulders and guided me inside.

'Whatever's the matter, love?' he asked.

I looked up into his eyes, full of genuine concern. I'm not sure why, but I felt safe with Chris; perhaps it was the masculinity he was giving off. He had an air about him that was consuming me. He felt like a real man, not a pathetic predatory animal like Madge's cousin, Richard fucking Ellis.

As I entered the flat, I wondered if Janet was ever at home, every fucker seemed to look after her kid except her.

Chris explained that Maureen had turned up about half an hour ago, telling Janet that some girl wanted a fight with her. Maureen hadn't wanted to fight, not without her big sister by her side, so Chris was left with baby Kevin.

I sat down and caught the faint smell of piss; for some

odd reason, it felt comforting this time around.

'You're Chris, aren't you?' he said warmly, 'I'll make you a brew.' His kindness made me well up again.

'He raped me,' I blurted out. I started talking and I couldn't stop. I told Chris everything that had happened; the alcohol, the attack, the walk home. I even admitted that I'd been attracted to Richard Ellis at first and that I'd led him on.

'The man's an animal,' he said, almost lost for words.

Chris made me a brew and I sat sipping it, sniffling and feeling sorry for myself.

'You could phone the dibble you know?' he said, looking at me seriously.

I didn't want the police involved; everyone would find out. I explained that my mum would kill me if she knew what I'd been up to. And that if my dad found out, he would kill him. Chris shook his head.

'If I were you, I wouldn't let your old man near him. He's a dodgy geezer that Richard Ellis. He's been coming here for ages and I'm sure he's up to something with our Janet, it knocks me sick, but there's nothing I can do, he'd have me fucking strung up. I know Janet's not his only bit on the side, he's got them all over; proper pervert he is.'

Janet and Maureen returned. Maureen gave me a look, a look I wasn't sure about, but I'd developed an obscure paranoia over the last twenty-four hours, so I shook it off. I could tell they'd had a good scrap by the way their hair was all dishevelled and Maureen's shirt had been ripped.

'Mum will fuckin' kill me,' she grinned.

We all laughed.

Maureen said she had to get home; I was disappointed.

'You're staying aren't you Chris?' Janet asked.

Sharing the same name, her brother and I both replied 'yes' at the same time which set everyone off laughing again.

Chapter 6

Richard Ellis

I couldn't get this one out of my mind.

I found out her name from my cousin. Christine Mellor.

She was cute, she was curvy, she was easy. I thought again about the way she'd come on to me, the way she'd wanted it. She would probably deny it, but I knew. She'd gone in the kitchen to touch herself; she was doing that while thinking about me. Horny bitch.

I thought about the look on her face when I'd given her another good fuck in the bushes. I fantasised about doing it again. I knew I would take her whenever I got the chance. She wanted it; she clearly wanted it.

Thinking about her turned me on. I needed a fuck. Shame I didn't know where Christine was right now. Maybe that dirty slag, Janet, would know where I could find her. If not, I'd just stick it up her instead; she was always wet for me.

I jumped in my car and headed back to that shithole estate.

Chapter 7

Christine Mellor

Maureen made her departure, and I sat chatting to Chris and Janet.

There was a knock on the door. I saw the unease in Janet's face and immediately guessed who it was.

I started to shake and it was painful to breathe. I put my head down and tried to shut out what was being said around me. It made me feel nauseous and I thought I was going to throw up.

Chris got up and walked down the long hall to the front door. He hesitated at the door, but then there was a second knock. He opened the front door abruptly. I could feel Richard's presence; I could even hear his breathing.

Janet came over and sat on the settee with me. 'I can't get out of his grip' she whispered. She held my hand, and as she did, I heard the thud of a fist.

I was rooted to that smelly settee.

Chris came into the room rubbing his hand. 'That'll teach the fucker,' he said.

I could tell he was worried about what the consequences of his actions might be. I ran over and threw my arms around him. He held me tight and then Janet joined us and the three of us hugged each other.

'He raped me,' I told Janet. She didn't look surprised.

'I believe you,' she said.

We sat down and spoke about the whole sordid ordeal; I was glad to get it off my chest.

Janet explained how he'd been turning up, demanding sex from her. She didn't like him coming over, but he'd give her money which she needed for baby Kevin's stuff. I felt sorry for her; she'd fallen into his slimy trap.

'Fuckin' animal,' Chris spat.

Baby Kevin appeared at the door, rubbing his beautiful green eyes. Janet picked him up and touched his nose with her nose.

'Let's go and have cuddles,' she said.

Turning to us she said, 'I'm going to go to bed.' She smiled sadly and gave me a big hug. I felt like I had an ally for life.

I snuggled up on the settee. Chris came over and put his arms around me. He looked straight into my eyes and said sincerely; 'I'll protect you, I won't leave your side.'

I believed him and his words filled me with happiness. At that moment, I knew Chris Parker would be part of my life forever.

He lay me down, grabbing an old blanket and throwing it over me. He kissed me on my head and told me to rest, then sat on a shabby, brown chair, that had a big rip down one side.

I was tired, but I couldn't sleep. I kept checking he was still there, and he was. I don't know what came over me, but I wanted him in a sexual way. Considering what I'd been through only twenty-four hours earlier, it was crazy, but it just felt so right.

I wanted him so badly that I questioned my own sanity. Maybe it was to wipe away what happened, but I had to have him.

I got up from the settee and walked towards him as he watched me silently. I climbed on to his knee and kissed him. He put his arms around me and kissed me back. I tentatively moved my hand down and stroked his erection through his jeans. I wanted him to know that I wanted him.

'Are you sure?' he asked. I nodded and kissed him again. He gently stood me up and stood in front of me as he carefully undressed me.

He took his jeans off and sat back down on the chair. I straddled him and he entered me slowly. This time the feeling was of warmth as he filled me with his cock. I moved very slowly up and down brushing my nipples in his face. He grabbed them gently with his mouth. I sat down hard on him. It was pain and it was pleasure rolled into one beautiful feeling. I gasped hard as we found our rhythm. He let out a quiet deep groan that made us both shudder.

'Wow,' he whispered, 'I didn't expect that.' He held me tightly to him, stroking the back of my neck.

'It just felt right,' I whispered.

Richard Ellis might have taken my virginity, but Chris Parker was the first man I had ever given myself to and it was perfect.

'Come on,' he said, 'let's get some sleep.'

We curled up on the settee with a blanket over us. I pretended it was forever because I wanted it to be forever.

Chapter 8

Richard Ellis

I couldn't' believe that scruffy cunt had lamped me in the face. I was so shocked that I had no time to react. If I had reacted, he'd have fucking known about it. I was fucking fuming. He could not do that to me; who did he think he was? I know Mellor was in there with him and wondered what was going on between them. She had better not be telling tales.

I had a flashback of her dancing in the kitchen with her hands down her knickers; it made my cock stir.

I knew she would be thinking about me. That slag Janet would get it as well; her kid was only clothed because of me. She owed me.

I sat in my car outside the flat and contemplated my next move. I was ready to kick her fucking door down but thought better of it. I didn't want to bring any attention to myself.

I turned the ignition on and sped off into the night, convinced they would hear the roar of my car and would know I meant business.

That slag with the kid had used me for money by opening her fucking legs. I can't believe I paid for it when I could get it anywhere for free. The other slag had led me on, teased me, and the very next night she was doing the same with him.

I drove around the estate. I needed to cut myself off from this shithole once and for all. I was making more money than any of this lot. There were plenty of ways to make extra money, and I was good at it. Taking bribes was easy, and I had a knack for getting people to do what I wanted.

I drove and I drove. The estate was vast and I could have driven around all night. The orange glow of the street lamps lit up the roads that ran through the estate, not all of them working, some of them flickering in hope.

After a while, I could hear the fucking milkman, the hum of his float and the rattle of the bottles on the back of it. He was driving at three miles an hour and getting right in my way, slowing me down. I overtook the fucker and passed a house I recognised. Maggie Lawrence lived there.

Maggie Lawrence was a bored housewife who I'd had my eye on as a potential for a shag. She was hardly a looker, but I could tell she was sad, lonely and gagging for a good fuck.

As I passed her house, I remembered a conversation we'd had not so long ago. Maggie had confided in me that her husband had been shagging some slag and she'd found out they had a kid together. That slag was Janet. In fact, that was how Janet got on my radar in the first place. I'd thought that if she was shagging married men, then I could get her to open her legs for me too. Plus, bringing up a bastard kid meant she'd be hard up for money; she was an easy target.

Last time I'd spoken to Maggie, she told me she thought her husband was still banging Janet whenever he got chance. 'If I could afford to burn that bitch to the ground, I would,' she told me.

As I recalled the conversation, I got an idea.

Chapter 9

Christine Mellor

I woke up in an unfamiliar bedroom. The walls were covered in woodchip and I was on a single bed, covered in blankets.

I felt a warmth next to me and realised where I was. Chris and I couldn't get comfortable on Janet's settee, so we'd snuck out in the middle of the night and gone to Chris's.

He put his arms around me, and I snuggled in tightly; we seemed to fit perfectly.

'How are you this morning? Bet it smells like Grimsby dock down there,' he joked.

I laughed and pretended to sniff under the covers. 'Smells like a summer's garden,' I giggled, and Chris went down to investigate.

Tingles went up and down my body as he expertly kissed me where I'd never been kissed before. He certainly knew what to do with his tongue. I arched my back as I gave in to the most powerful orgasm I'd ever had. He came up laughing, all pleased with himself.

'What are you doing today?' he asked.

I racked my brain and then remembered that my mum had got me a job at the nearby cake factory, known locally as 'the bakery.' It was my first shift this evening.

'I'm starting my new job,' I told him, feeling proud of myself. He listened as I explained what I was going to be doing and how nervous I felt because the women who worked there were a feisty bunch.

He asked if my parents would be worried about me, and I blushed a little. I was nearly sixteen for god sake, but yeah, they would probably be wondering where I was. It wasn't unusual for me not to come home, I often dossed down at one of my mates. My mum would go nuts if she found out I'd stayed with a boy though. I shoved it to the back of my mind and carried on enjoying the moment. I'd deal with that later. I would say I'd stayed at Maureen's house. It wasn't a lie since Maureen did live there. I would just leave out the detail of whose room I'd stayed in.

Chris went to the bathroom, and I looked out his bedroom window. He lived almost opposite Janet's flat, but the nearly-finished motorway was now coming between them. You could just see the flats through the saplings that had been planted.

I saw a police car coming down the road with its blue light flashing and its orange stripe clashing with the early morning sun. My stomach lurched as it pulled up outside Chris's house. I watched anxiously as two uniformed policemen got out with two other men in suits. I couldn't believe what I was seeing.

One of the men was Richard Ellis. He was dressed smartly and had an air of authority about him. He looked straight up to the window as if he knew I was watching him. I dived on to the bed and under the covers as if they could protect me. What the fuck did he want? Surely he wasn't going to arrest Chris for punching him after what he'd done to me?

There was a tiny knock on the bedroom door. I didn't know what to do, so I just stared at the door until Maureen finally let herself in.

'Our Chris has just told me to come up to you,' she whispered. 'What happened last night after I left?'

'What are the police doing here?' I said, completely ignoring Maureen's question.

'They want to speak to mum and dad, but dad's not in yet, so they're waiting for him.'

I was feeling claustrophobic and desperate to leave, but I didn't want him to see me. I was the cause of all this, why did he want to speak to their mum and dad?

Chris popped his head around the door; 'You ok?' he looked concerned.

'What does he want?' I asked.

'Fuck knows. They're not saying anything until my dad

gets back. He's probably just being a cocky fuck and trying to intimidate me. Don't worry.'

He smiled at me and then went back downstairs.

I heard Mr Parker arrive and there was a commotion of some sorts. I didn't understand what was happening, but it didn't sound good; my stomach was turning over and I was feeling sicker and sicker by the minute.

Maureen sat next to me on the bed and we were squeezing each other's hands tightly.

'What the fuck does he want?' I asked as if Maureen would know. She just shook her head.

Then there was an almighty scream from downstairs. Maureen and I looked into each other's eyes and we knew without speaking that it was a scream of death.

We ran downstairs to find Mrs Parker sobbing inconsolably. Her husband was trying to calm her down as Chris sat sobbing with his hands in his head. He looked straight at me, his eyes piercing my soul as he sobbed. 'They're dead! Our Janet and baby Kevin are dead.'

Chapter 10

Richard Ellis

I got what I needed and headed back to the slag's flat. I was going to make sure they perished; they deserved it. That Christine Mellor should be mine. She gave me her virginity. He'd turned her against me.

When I got back to the flat, the door was unlocked making it even easier for me to make what I was going to do look like an accident.

I had to be careful not to wake anybody. It wouldn't do me any good right now to get caught.

I'd taken some paraffin from my mother's shed and picked up some matches. I was originally going to pour it through the letterbox and torch the shithole, but they'd made it so much easier by leaving the door open.

As I slipped quietly into the hallway, I realised how familiar I was with this place. That dirty piece of meat had always been willing. She came at a cost though, and that's what was fucking infuriating me. That, and the thought of her wanker of a brother getting it on with the fucking virgin slag.

To the left, there was a doorway which I knew was where she washed her clothes in a huge sink. There were always clothes soaking while a pile of smelly clothes sat on the floor waiting for their turn. I went in, shut the door quietly behind me and calmly lit a cigarette. I poured the smallest amount of paraffin onto the pile of dirty washing and threw the cig onto it. It immediately went up in flames, and my next thought was to get out quick.

As I left the washroom, I saw that fucking kid, Kevin, standing in the hall rubbing his eyes.

I couldn't let him die in a fire. The others, no problem, but not a little kid. I grabbed him and quietly left the scene. All hell would soon break loose as the flat went up in flames; just another fire caused by a careless smoker.

I threw the kid in the car and sped off. At first, he was silent, probably still half asleep, then he started to whine. What the fuck was I going to do with him?

My first thought was to throw the little fucker back into the flat, but it would be too late now; the fire would be in full swing.

Then I had an idea. Maggie Lawrence.

The cogs in my brain were whirring fast. There was no denying that the kid definitely had an Irish look to him just like his dad. In fact, stick him in a room with the rest of those filthy Lawrence kids and nobody would notice the difference. Maggie's husband, the kid's father, was a raging alcoholic who probably didn't have a fucking clue how many children he had anyway.

It was perfect. I swung the car around and headed towards Maggie Lawrence's house.

She owed me big time; she would have to have the kid. I'd done her a massive favour; I'd done what she'd asked. She'd have her pathetic husband back; well, at least until he found his next bit on the side. She owed me for sure.

It was getting late as I pulled up to their house. I could hear sirens blaring in the distance. 'Too late fuckers; they'll all be dead.' I clasped my hands together and shook them as I inhaled the taste of victory.

The lights were off, but I could see white flashes behind the curtains which indicated that someone was watching telly inside.

I hoped that he wasn't there; it was a risk for sure. As luck would have it though, Maggie answered the door.

I looked at her face closely. I could see that she was once a pretty woman, but life was dragging her down along with her kids and her rat of a husband. She probably hadn't had a proper fuck for years and that thought was enough to cause a stir in my pants. The thought of fucking a frustrated, frumpy housewife turned me on.

'What do you want?' she whispered. Her confusion made her look vulnerable, but she wasn't stupid. I stared at her intensely.

'I did what you asked,' I told her calmly.

'What did you do?' she said, shaking her head in confusion.

We'd only had a few interactions, but I knew how to get women and girls to trust me. I could pick up on their insecurities, their weaknesses and their strengths, and use it against them. They'd confide in me, open their hearts and then their legs as well. By the time I'd got my way with them, they were so ensnared, so wrapped up in me, that they'd forget about their own self-worth. They'd forget that life was even happening around them.

It wasn't just a game for me; I had to destroy them because the more I took them down, the stronger I became. I needed the victory, it enabled me to live, and If they didn't give me that, then they would suffer.

'What have you done? she repeated.

She fucking knew.

'You wanted her wiping out. You said if you could afford it, you'd have her burnt alive.'

The look of sheer panic on her face as she registered what I was telling her was a sight to behold. I took a deep breath as I went in for the kill.

'Don't worry. I don't want paying in cash, but I do need you to keep something for me.'

She went to shut the door in my face, but I quickly stopped her. 'Too late for all that now love, you owe me. I did what you wanted.'

'Jesus! I just said it in passing. I didn't mean it,' she whispered.

'Did you say it?'

'Well,' she muttered.

'Did you say it?' I was serious now. I had no time for fucking about; I needed rid of this fucking kid.

'I...err... I was...' she stuttered.

'Wait there.'

Seconds later, I was back at the door with the kid asleep in my arms.

'Here,' I said and thrust him towards her. 'He'll blend in;

no one will know the difference,'

'What the fuck?' she said staring at him.

'You will never tell a soul that I was here. If you do, I will start investigating you for murder and kidnap, and I will win. You know I will win.'

She nodded her head vigorously. I could see her mind doing overtime, weighing up the situation, but she would do it.

She was wavering. I went in for the kill.

'I'll help where I can,' I smiled. 'It'll give me a reason to visit you more often and keep you company.'

I touched her breast ever so softly so that my fingers caught her nipples under her flimsy cheap blouse. I could see her cheeks flush as she quickly looked behind her. 'If you'd like me to?' I said.

I had her now. She was so desperate to get her lips around my cock that she'd take in a wild tiger if I asked.

'Now, take the kid and do what you can. I'll be back soon.'

I handed her the sleeping child, and she reluctantly took him from me. 'What's his name?'

'Peter,' I lied.

She visibly softened once she had a name. I saw her hold him close to her breast, and I thought about her nipples getting hard under her blouse.

Chapter 11

Christine Mellor

Since getting the news about Janet and Kevin, the Parkers' lives had been torn in two.

They'd died in a house fire caused by a cigarette. I would never understand or truly believe it. For all Janet's faults, she was always careful around her son. I couldn't believe that she would have got out of bed for a cigarette after we'd left. She'd been fast asleep. They both had. I couldn't get that night or the one before it out of my mind. I felt like it was all my fault. My god, would it ever leave me? The lump in my throat felt like a permanent fixture these days.

I couldn't help thinking about the fact that I could have been there, as could Chris. If we had settled on the settee and hadn't snuck back to his house, we'd both have been burnt alive too. Or would we? Maybe we'd have woken up and raised the alarm. Maybe we'd have got Janet and Kevin out alive and they'd be with us now. I could barely bring myself to think about it without bursting into tears.

Naturally, Chris's mum and dad had taken it badly, but we all pulled together as a team and looked after one another. It wasn't long before I was practically living at the Parker house. It didn't happen intentionally; it was the circumstances. Chris needed me, and I needed him. I couldn't bear to be apart from him.

My mum wasn't happy about it, but she just had to accept it, given what had gone on. Even she wouldn't be daft enough to pull me out from an injured pack for fear of being attacked.

My job at the factory had been delayed. They had let me start a few days later since I could've been burnt to death in a fire. It was still bad timing, but I needed it for financial reasons and to give me something to focus on. As it turned out, I started on my sixteenth birthday. It's not like it was going to be a happy birthday anyway.

The older women ruled the roost, while us younger ones did as we were told. You soon learnt that if you were quiet and didn't speak up for yourself, you wouldn't have a leg to stand on. Yet, if you answered back, you got the dressing down of your life.

Some of the supervisors were men, as well as a few loaders who would take the boxes of cakes on their forklift trucks. Other than that, it was a very woman orientated environment and everybody knew each other. Generations of families worked there. It wasn't uncommon for an employee to work alongside her sister, mother, daughter, cousin or neighbour. We were a close-knit community.

The women worked hard, harder than the men. They made those fucking cakes like their lives depended on it. Us youngsters didn't quite have that drive to begin with, but we would quickly learn because if you didn't keep up, you were made to feel weak and you had to take the insults.

The jam tarts were the most difficult to work on. You had to be made of fucking steel. The number of hands that got burnt on the red-hot jam left a lot of the women walking around in agony.

Me, my mum and my sister, Gill, worked there on the same shift. The money was good, and the staff shop had loads of bargains. Working there gave me some time away from what was going on in my head. I was either too busy working hard or laughing with the girls or sticking up for myself. There was always something going on to take my mind off the fact that I had been raped.

I knew that I would never forgive myself for putting myself in that position and knew it was best kept hidden. I never wanted to give my mum that feeling of helplessness, the feeling of guilt and the feeling of shame. No, I would take this one with me. Only my Chris knew, and Janet, god rest her soul.

Richard knew, of course, but I doubted he'd be shouting about it. I shook my head. I had to get that man out of my mind.

I couldn't shake the feeling that he'd caused the fire.

That he'd come back for me that night; not satisfied with taking my virginity and my dignity, he wanted my life too.

The idea of him frightened me to death. It was so bad that I couldn't even talk to Chris about it, even though he probably felt the same as I did.

We had talked briefly about going to the police with the whole story, but knew it was pointless.

'He fuckin' works for them,' Chris had said, exasperated by the whole shit situation we had found ourselves in. 'He's dirty as they come and he'll do anything to prove us wrong. As much as I hate to say it, he's good at playing people. We don't stand a chance and we'll come off worse.'

We had made a pact there and then that we wouldn't talk about Richard Ellis again and that we'd just try and get on with our lives.

Something else played on my mind. Baby Kevin. I'd not spoken to Chris about it, but there had been no reports of his little body being found. It was bizarre, but I was almost afraid to ask. Janet was buried, and at the funeral, they mentioned her son, but his body had never been released. I don't know if it was any of my business, but it was all so confusing.

Chapter 12

Richard Ellis

If she hadn't danced like that in the kitchen, and if that wanker hadn't punched me in the face, none of this would have happened. It was their fault; the pair of them killed Chris Parker's sister.

Janet was nothing but a waste of fucking space anyway. I wasn't sorry. It was done now and there was no going back. I'd wanted to kill the lot of them, but it was even better this way. They would have to live with the guilt of what had happened, and I'd get another go with Christine Mellor.

I'd been watching her. If I got the chance, I'd give her another good fucking. I knew exactly where she lived and that she was working in the large cake factory on the industrial estate. She was practically living with that fucking wanker, Chris Parker. I'd stay out the way when he was there, but I would get her back one day, I knew I would.

I sat outside the factory again. It was a lovely summer's evening, and the sun cast an orange glow over everything.

The women and girls came out wearing blue overalls and hair nets. They were all chattering, probably gossiping about some poor bastard that wasn't there. That's what they were like these factory women, loud mouth gossips who wouldn't think twice of shouting you down in front of anyone. They cackled away like a coven of witches.

There she was.

She was following the crowd toward some bloke's car. The wanker was probably selling bags of goodies out of his boot. The cacklers would buy anything if it was cheap enough, from socks to knickers to toffee.

Today was Thursday which was payday. For this lot, that would mean buying a load of shit from a car boot and splashing out on fish and chips for tea. By the time they got home, they'd have no fucking money left.

She was becoming a cackler, a loud mouth. I could tell

by her demeanour that she had grown in confidence over the last few months. I bet she still thought of me daily though.

She had no idea I knew her every move. I tried to plan it so that I would bump into her, but it was difficult to get her on her own. She worked the same shift as her mum and sister, and her dad would pick them up from work each evening. I could see him tonight waiting patiently in his car while his three vultures went through some dodgy geezer's boot.

'I'll give you 50p for all those bags of sweets,' I heard Christine say.

'Fuck off Chrissie. Your teeth would fall out.'

I looked at the bloke selling shit from his boot. I had a good mind to report him for selling knock-off gear, but he was the least of my worries. Instead, I focused on her. I could take her away from all this, give her a proper life. I knew what she needed and I was the only one who could give it to her properly.

Chapter 13

Christine Mellor

I needed to have a conversation with Chris; despite our pact, it would involve discussing Richard Ellis.

I'd realised that the recent bouts of sickness I'd been having weren't down to stress after all, just as the weight gain wasn't down to overeating the cakes from work.

I was pregnant.

I hadn't had a period since the night I was raped. Even though I'd slept with Chris the night after, I knew it would be Richard's. Chris would know it too. He wasn't daft.

The stress was becoming too much to bear and I had to make a decision. Should I tell Chris it was his and hope for the best? Or should I tell him the truth and hope that he didn't leave me alone with a baby?

I'd settled for the latter in my head. I would always be honest with him; he was my hero, my best friend. Yes, I would always tell him the truth. I just needed to find the right time.

I'd tell him tonight, I decided as I left work.

Mum and Gill had already clocked out and were waiting for me in dad's car. I constantly felt sick at the minute and it was slowing me down.

As I walked through the corridors of the main building, I saw Richard standing there. I had to walk past him, so I tried to do so with my head held high.

'Alright Christine?' He was so arrogant. His handsome face now seemed so very ugly to me. It was sly; I could see that now. There was something non-symmetrical about it. If you looked closely, one half had a smile to it from his eyes to his mouth. The other side looked evil, with dead eyes and a downward smile. I hated his face.

'You better keep quiet about me, do you understand?' he said. His voice was threatening, but his face gave nothing away.

He knew I was scared and I could tell that he enjoyed the fear that was flowing through my body. I couldn't answer him even if I wanted to as my throat was so dry, it prevented me from speaking. The thought that the child in my belly could be his made me feel queasy and I instinctively touched my stomach.

He stared at me and I felt his gaze rest on my belly.

'I miss nothing, and I know everything,' he said smiling, and with that, he walked off.

I was relieved to see that my dad was waiting in his usual spot for us. I was full of trepidation when I opened the car door and dived on the back seat.

'What's up with your face?' dad asked.

'Nothing's up,' I answered.

I looked around as though I could feel Richard's eyes upon me. I knew he was near; I knew he could see me. He couldn't possibly know about the baby, could he? I shuddered as I closed the car door. Would I ever feel safe again?

Chapter 14

Richard Ellis

I was restless; I couldn't sleep. I needed a release, but I needed a release with a difference. I'd been spending too much time with council estate scum. It was time to visit my wife.

Helen was mine whenever I wanted her; she was obsessed with me. I was all she had; I made sure of it.

She lived in a little village called Wilmslow. Although it was only a few miles from the estate, it was completely different. The people who lived there had money, nice cars and stunning houses.

Helen's parents had left her a beautiful, big house when they died. They'd also left her an abundance of money which meant she wanted for nothing.

I'd worked with Helen's dad before he and his wife were killed in a car crash. I took Helen under my wing, looked after her, made sure that she didn't want or need anybody else. I became her whole world.

She had given birth to two sons. I knew that she had never been with anyone else, so they had to be mine. She depended entirely on me, so she just stayed put, looking after her two offspring in her beautiful home. It was perfect.

I hadn't seen her for a while as I had been so wrapped up in all the shit I was dealing with. I decided to pay her a visit.

Half an hour later, I was in the village of Wilmslow. It wasn't too late, but the pubs were shut. The evening was warm, and I hadn't bothered to put a jacket on.

Helen's house was built in the middle of some woods with the River Bollin flowing through it. Wildlife often came to forage in what was a magnificent garden. There was a half a mile dirt track leading up to the house. A few cobbles left here and there made it a bumpy ride. Dense trees on either side of the road made it difficult to see, especially in the darkness of the night.

Two stone posts held the old iron gates in place. Bricks were missing where a lever had been installed; when you tugged it downwards, a bell rang in the house. All I had to do was pull it and she was mine.

I would never commit to staying here full time. The way to a woman's heart is to make her feel insecure, make her feel like she isn't good enough for you. I didn't want it to look like I only wanted the house. I needed her to think that I didn't need or want any of it. I paid my way with her, spent money on her and gave her money for the two kids.

As I tugged at the lever, I saw a light go on inside. She appeared at the front door, then walked across the big courtyard in her silk dressing gown. A row of tall gas lights lit the way from the house to the gate.

Her dark face and jet-black hair were visible in the moonlight. She looked like an African princess, her features enhanced by the gas lights. She was certainly classy, and she was getting It tonight.

She smiled shyly then wagged her finger at me cheekily. An indication that she wasn't happy with me because I'd not been for a while.

As I got out of the car, I felt genuinely pleased to see her. She looked fresh and clean and smelt delicious, not like any of the others. I could tell she was happy to see me too.

Helen had a certain aura about her that made her special. She was a shy looking woman with large brown puppy dog eyes that looked like they would fill with tears if she was offended. She was not a slag; she had never had any other boyfriends, or so she told me.

She was mine, all mine, and when nobody else was around to give me my much-needed supply, I always had her.

We went through the big, wooden front door, across the large square hallway and into a huge kitchen with stone floors. The lounge was on the right, and there was a wide wooden staircase to the left. There was no carpet on the stairs, just beautiful stained and polished wood.

Helen didn't have a particularly high sex drive, but she

was always ready for sex with me. I could tell by the hunger in her eyes just how much she wanted me.

I picked her up off her feet and carried her up the stairs as she giggled and kissed my face.

I sat on the big double bed and watched as her pert nipples became visible through the silk night-gown she was wearing. What I was feeling was torture, it was a feeling of yearning that I rarely felt with any woman. I wanted her as much as she wanted me, and I wanted us to enjoy it together, I wanted us to be one.

She stripped off and I was hard as a rock. She pulled my trousers off, and my cock burst out of my pants. I positioned her on her back and slowly kissed her bushy, triangular-shaped pubic hair. It was thick and I teased it with my fingers, pulling at it softly before I pushed her legs open with my head. I licked her pussy, smelling her and breathing her in as I did. I loved the warm wet juice against my tongue. It felt like silk. She groaned and writhed with pleasure.

My dick throbbed so damn hard, I felt like I was going to come while she was in my mouth.

'Do you like that Helen?' I asked. She moaned, but it wasn't loud enough, so I asked her again, louder this time. 'Do you like that Helen?'

She murmured that she loved it. She must have because she arched her back and throbbed hard into my mouth; her pussy almost doubled in size as she reached orgasm.

I rolled on my back and pulled her on top of me. I lowered Helen onto my hardness holding her hips as I slowly pushed her onto it. I looked up at her pert breast and her dark brown nipples jiggling up and down. I erupted and released my load hard inside her.

That was exactly what I had needed.

I felt her slide next to me and put her arms around me, but the moment I came for had gone and I didn't want the intimacy now. I rolled over, turning my back on her. She was just a nobody now. I needed my sleep.

Chapter 15

Christine Mellor

It was good of dad to pick us up every night from work, and after tonight's encounter with Richard, I felt particularly grateful.

The beige leather seats were cool on my bare legs, and the radio comforted me as it crooned away. It was always at the same volume; he never turned it up. Me and Gill found out he glued the volume knob so that it couldn't be altered.

'Chippy?' mum asked Gill and me.

'Er, I'm going to Chris's tonight,' I murmured from the back seat.

She wasn't happy that I was practically living with the Parkers. It just wasn't the done thing; she would fucking die if she knew we shared a bed. I'd told her that I was sharing with Maureen.

Day after day and night after night, mum would take any opportunity to remind me that my home was with them. Maybe if she knew half of what had gone on she might have let up once in a while.

Not missing a beat, she piped up; 'We'll pick Chris up on the way, he can have a chippy tea with us too.'

I was in no mood to argue or re-arrange the complexities of it in my head. It was too much effort and I couldn't be bothered, so I decided to go with it. It just meant that I had to deal with the pregnancy alone a little longer.

We drove from the busy industrial estate towards where we lived. There were lots of factories, but the smell of cakes generally filled the air.

Next to where we worked was Wylex where they made electrical components. The women that worked there were worse than us. They'd call a spade a spade even if it wasn't a spade.

We turned onto a wide road that had rows of shops along one side. On the other side were the local swimming baths.

The front of the dome-shaped building was made of glass, and you could see people enjoying their swim.

'What will Chris have?' Mum asked, not letting the idea drop.

'Don't know,' I shrugged, 'fish, chips and mushy peas I suppose.'

'And what about you?'

'Same.'

'What the hell is up with you?' She yelled from her front seat. She was getting impatient now.

'Nothing mum, I just wasn't expecting chippy that's all.'

'It's Thursday, Chrissie. It's payday, what were you expecting? Don't the Parkers have a chippy on a Thursday?'

We pulled up outside the chip shop. I wasn't going to argue. I wouldn't win, and besides, my mind was elsewhere.

I sat in the car while they stood in the very long queue inside the chippy. Kids were running in and out; youngsters were pressing their faces on the hot glass, staring at the fish and fritters cooked in golden batter. Others came out carrying their fish and chips wrapped in newspaper.

'Do you want a buttered bread Chrissie?' Mum shouted from the door. I nodded my head. I don't know why as I didn't really feel like eating anything right now.

I felt shit. This was a normal Thursday night, but I wasn't in the mood.

I saw Madge walking up the road; she was probably heading home. She was alone, so I rapped on the window and waved as she walked passed the car.

She saw me but didn't look too pleased; she never did since the night I was raped. I was annoyed by her change in attitude. I hadn't done anything to upset her; because of the mood I was in right now, I felt like I needed to tell her.

I got out the car.

'Hey, Madge, you alright? I've not seen you for a while?'

She was certainly caught off guard. She sighed.

'Look Chrissie; I told you that my cousin was bad news. Don't think for a moment that I don't know what's going on?'

I remembered his threat. I was afraid to ask what she was referring to; the rape, the fire, what did she know?

'I just want to keep out of it,' she said. 'He told me that if there is any contact between us then there will be consequences and I don't want that.'

She looked around her as though he might be listening; she lowered her voice.

'Me and Jon are having a baby, and I just don't want any trouble. It wasn't planned so we've got a lot to sort out.'

I felt my face flush hot.

'Err, yeah, I know what you mean.'

She glared at me but didn't say anything.

'When are you due?' I asked curiously.

'Seven months,' she said and smiled. She looked around again. 'You just take care and watch out Chrissie; he's watching you.'

I shuddered at the very thought of him.

Madge turned and scurried off. I got back into the car just as Mum and Gill returned with their packets of chips.

'Right, let's go and get Chris,' said mum.

The smell of the vinegar on the fish and chips usually made my mouth water but not tonight. Tonight, I could only taste fear and no amount of food would wash it away.

Chapter 16

Richard Ellis

I woke up; she was still sleeping. My disdain for her had returned now she'd given me what I wanted.

It must have been early or the kids would have been awake. I couldn't be arsed with the kids. I needed to get ready and do a normal day's work. I needed to get out of here.

I couldn't be bothered being the dutiful dad. They adored me, but I was far too busy to entertain them. That's what she was for. I wasn't happy with the way she brought them up; she was far too soft on them. They might as well have been little girls; they certainly wouldn't grow up to be proper men like their father at this rate.

She stirred; 'Morning,' she whispered, smiling at me lovingly.

Her constant good manners and respect for me always made me feel good.

'Morning,' I muttered. 'I've got to go.'

'So soon,' she whined, 'you've not even seen the boys.'

Who did she think she was? How dare she make demands on me? I had to go to work; I didn't have time to mess about with the 'boys'.

'Do you really think I have time to waste playing with children?' I asked sternly. 'What will you do while I look after your sons? Where were you thinking of going?'

I enjoyed the trepidation in her face. I could always twist things to make her think that I was right, and she always did.

'Have you got your eye on someone else?' I asked her.

I watched her as she attempted to squirm her way out of it.

'No!' she exclaimed, 'I love you and only you. You're my world; you know that Richard.'

Mission accomplished.

That would teach her to whine about the boys again.

I left. She was happy that I believed she didn't have anyone else, relieved that it had stopped at that. She knew that if she'd said one more wrong word, I'd have unleashed hell on her.

After work, I had things to do. I needed to check on Maggie Lawrence and make sure the kid was ok. I should just forget about them both, but the thought of her vulnerability and how she felt responsible for Janet's death excited me. I'd done the right thing leaving the kid with the Lawrence's. I couldn't have let the little fucker die.

When I arrived, Maggie and her clan were out in the garden. I made sure the husband wasn't around before I entered. Her kids were digging in the mud with spoons and throwing soil at one another. A couple of them had old washing up liquid bottles filled with water and were creating a filthy mud bath.

Peter sat in the corner on his own not making eye contact with anyone. It was apparent that Maggie had no interest in him and it actually made me feel a bit sorry for him. He hadn't asked to be snatched away and put in another environment with all these people. On the other hand, the little fucker would be dead now if it wasn't for me. He'd be grateful for it one day; I'd make sure of it.

Maggie looked up from her chair and seemed almost pleased to see me. As she walked over to open the gate, she became conscious of her dishevelled appearance.

'Have you come to take him away?' she asked hopefully.

'Nope, that's not gonna happen,' I responded. 'How can it when you ordered for his mother to be murdered?'

She shook her head in disbelief. 'I didn't mean it.'

I chuckled; 'Perhaps you should think before you speak.'

'What am I going to do with him? He's cried constantly; I've not slept in days.'

'You do look tired,' I said, feigning sympathy.

She almost burst into tears at the acknowledgement.

'Come on,' I said gently as I guided her into the house. 'The older ones will look after the children. You need five minutes.'

'I can't do that,' she protested but put up little resistance.

I led her into the living room. She looked haggard; no wonder her husband had been fucking about. I doubt he had paid her any attention in years.

We sat down, and I gently stroked her hand.

'I'll help you with Peter,' I reassured her. 'I'll take him out, and I'll pay towards his keep and upbringing.

'Thank you,' she said, sounding grateful. I decided to test just how grateful she was.

'Take that apron off,' I instructed.

Without question, she stood up and untied the strings from behind her waist. She consciously moved her hair out of her face.

'That's better,' I said, 'you really are beautiful, you know.'

She put her head down embarrassed, clearly not used to receiving any compliments. This was going to be easier than I thought.

I stood up next to her and started to push the bottom of her skirt upwards gently and softly. The feeling of my hands on her thighs was making her quiver. I could almost smell her juicing up for me.

I stopped, and she stood there looking helpless, not really knowing what to do next. She bent over the old green settee to check on the kids outside.

'They're ok, aren't they?' I said. Again, I rubbed her skirt up her legs. She actually groaned and her face started to relax.

'When was the last time you had any attention?' I asked her.

'I don't remember,' she responded honestly.

I pulled her hand slowly to the bulge in my trousers.

'Well, you need some Maggie. It will make you feel better.'

She didn't take her hand off my cock. Instead, she started to rub it. I moved her to where I wanted her and bent her over the settee.

I pulled her skirt up and her big panties down. They had

seen better days, but they actually turned me on.

I stood back to take in the view; her white arse looked virginal. I could see she was already wet and it was clear she was more than ready to take me.

Before I slipped my hard cock into her, I knelt down and gave her a real treat. I licked her pussy slowly from behind, opening her up with my fingers while I did so. I didn't have to ask if she liked it because she pushed herself hard onto my face and came in a way I knew she hadn't done for a long time, if ever.

I stood up and slid my cock hard between the cheeks of her arse. She winced. Jesus! It felt brand new. Old Mr Lawrence didn't know what he was fucking missing; this was heaven on a plate. I pulled my cock out and ejaculated all over her white arse.

'Do you feel better now?' I asked.

She was in a daze, I could tell.

'That was... err... my husband never makes me... err... I've never –' she stopped and looked toward the door.

I turned around and saw Peter standing there. I had a feeling he'd been there the entire time. He wasn't much more than a baby, but I still felt uncomfortable.

'Get that fucking kid out,' I demanded, and she jumped up quickly and took him back out into the garden.

I left it a minute then followed them. I slipped her some money; it wasn't that I was paying for her services, but I had promised to give her money for Peter.

'You already look better,' I smiled. She smiled too; a pathetic smile that proved all a woman ever needed was a good fucking.

Chapter 17

Christine Mellor

I still hadn't spoken to Chris about being pregnant. In fact, I'd not spoken to anyone about it, and I was starting to feel more and more anxious. I needed to have the conversation, but there was never a time when we were alone or a time when it was appropriate.

It was Saturday night and I was supposed to be going for a work's night out. The girls at the bakery had a pot which they paid money into weekly. Once a year they'd have a big night out and everyone who contributed was welcome. You always got a few who wanted to come at the last minute. That was when the bickering and bitching would start about who had paid what and when. It was a logistical and emotional nightmare.

This year's night out was being held at The Golden Garter. It was quite an upmarket place not far from home. They had a different live act performing each week, sometimes a band or singer, other times a comedian. There were big burly bouncers on the doors because at times things got a bit rowdy. The trouble wasn't usually caused by men from the estate but by the women, especially if there was a male act on. They'd throw themselves at the acts, throw their knickers and scruffy bras and even fight over them.

Tonight's act was Gene Pitney; it had been the talk of the factory for months, but I really wasn't in the mood. I didn't want to go. My bloody mother wasn't giving me a choice though. She was insistent that me and Gill went and that we all got ready together at home.

I looked down at my belly and made a pact never to be so controlling when I became a mother.

I immediately felt sick. It was hard to admit there was a child in there and I wasn't even sure what would happen to it yet. I wasn't ready to be a mum, controlling or not.

The younger girls all wore long dresses, including Gill and me. Ours were the same style but different colours; hers was red and mine was blue. They had a huge V neck which showed my cleavage.

I wore my hair in a ruffle on top of my head; Gill had a go at what looked like a beehive. The amount of hair lacquer she must have used to keep it up could have kept the hairspray companies in business for years.

Mum wore some sort of two-piece suit that looked ridiculous. It was navy blue with white piping down the front of it. She looked like a fucking sailor but who was I to judge?

'This was your Nana's suit, you know? Do you like it?' She was brushing it down proudly.

I could barely respond. I actually wanted to laugh. 'Yes mum, I do,' I lied. It was easier to keep the peace.

'You've not been in The Garter before have you Chrissie?' Mum asked, knowing that I hadn't.

'No mum,' I answered.

'Have you Gill?' She moved from sister to sister just like that. Never really interested in the answer, more interested in hearing her own gob.

Gill looked at me in disbelief and mocked my reply in a 'we stand together' way that made me smile.

'No mum.'

We both giggled and I felt unusually close to her. I wondered if I should confide in her about everything, but very quickly had second thoughts. Even though we hardly spoke, we loved each other, and she would be devastated if she knew that I'd been raped and might be carrying my rapist's child.

'Why don't you wear my necklace tonight. It's only cheap, but it will go with your eyes,' said Gill, pulling a necklace out of her top drawer and putting it around my neck.

My eyes filled up. I wanted my old life back, but then I wouldn't have Chris. Then again, I might not have Chris much longer anyway once I told him I was having Richard

Ellis's baby.

I felt like I was going to be sick again.

'You ok Chrissie?' Gill asked.

I paused for a moment and just as I was about to reveal all, mum burst into the room.

'Come on girls! For god sake, your dad is in the car waiting.'

'He's sat in the car so he doesn't have to listen to her,' Gill muttered, and I burst out laughing.

And so, off we went to watch Gene Pitney with a load of loud mouth factory women.

I was shocked at how lavish The Golden Garter was inside. It had luxurious, thick carpets and there was a coat attendant who gave you a raffle ticket for your coat.

Through the glass partition between the club and the foyer, I could see how beautifully decorated it was. Barmen were running around in green and gold striped waistcoats.

I couldn't believe how posh it was. It looked like any other building from the outside.

There were dozens of round tables, each with an ashtray for a centrepiece. They also had little lamps on them which were really pretty. The air was filled with cigarette smoke and everything was hazy. There was a dance floor headed up with a stage that looked very impressive, all sparkly with a set of drums ready and waiting for the act that needed them. Big plaster goddesses sat on each side of the stage.

The foyer was the designated meeting place, and it was starting to get busy as more and more women from the bakery congregated there. We were waiting for Gwen as she had the tickets.

The girls were noisy as they came together. The jokes between women could become vicious, especially these women.

'Hey love, did you get that off the market? How much?'

'Was Lizzie at The Lion not selling them the other week? In fact, I think she was giving them away.'

'You should have worn your fuckin' hairnet. Your hair looks better at work.'

'Look better in brown that would Linda.'

'I've brought my own booze; not paying these fuckin' prices.'

'How you getting home Barbara? Our John said he'd come at half eleven. I'm not staying here all fuckin' night.'

'Hope they serve the food before the act. I'm fuckin' starving. I've not eaten all day; been saving myself for this?'

And so the comments went on. If they weren't throwing insults around, they were moaning about one thing or another.

Suddenly, Barbara Bentley turned her attention to me; 'Hey Chrissie, you're piling it on, aren't you? You're not up the duff are you?'

I nearly fainted on the spot. The look mum gave me said it all. 'You better fuckin' not be lady, or I'll be round at that Parker's house demanding some answers.'

Gill came to my rescue; 'How fuckin' rude are you?' she said, staring at Barbara Bentley in disgust. 'Do you know how much trouble you could have just caused?'

'Sorry,' Barbara said, 'I just thought she'd put on a bit of weight.'

'She's barely fuckin' sixteen years old; she's still getting her curves. You'll make her self-conscious with those kinds of comments. Keep your fucking opinions to yourself.'

Barbara looked offended and I was worried it would get out of hand.

'Stop!' I said. 'It doesn't matter. Let's just get in and get our table. No harm done.'

Everyone calmed down and their attention turned to Gwen who had finally arrived with the tickets.

'You are, aren't you?' Gill whispered to me, her face full of concern.

'Yeah,' I admitted, 'but, please, not here.' She nodded, and we headed inside the club.

They'd reserved five tables for our group. I was sitting with Gill, my mum and a few other women who were old dragons. Thank god I wasn't with Barbara Bentley though.

A few tables were reserved for the local bank workers.

They were snotty cows for sure, probably never seen a jam tart in their lives, they'd certainly never burnt their hands on one.

The night began and the booze started flowing. Some women had stashed alcohol in their handbags so they didn't have to pay. There was a hefty risk of them being thrown out if they were caught, but they didn't care.

Mum was sneaking me drinks. I was sure she was doing it to test me, find out if I was pregnant after all. I didn't want her to know my secret, so I sipped away at them pretending to enjoy myself.

I was beginning to feel a bit tipsy and needed to get my head together; last time I felt like this, I'd gotten myself into trouble.

I went to the toilets to have five minutes. The toilets were jammed packed with women. There were women reapplying their lipstick, re-doing their hair, some just staring at themselves while having conversations with a toilet door. They were all chatting and bitching about their mates. The gossip was rife and if you stayed long enough, you'd have a very different view of the people you were sat next to outside.

I finally got a cubicle and locked the door. I leant back on the toilet while I had a wee. I could have quite happily spent the rest of the night there away from it all. I was missing Chris and decided that I'd phone him afterwards to pick me up. I'd noticed a pay phone in the foyer.

I came out of the cubicle to find two women complaining about their husbands. One was moaning about how he didn't do 'it' to her anymore. She thought he was getting it from somewhere else and it wouldn't be the first time.

The other was saying she had found someone else to do 'it' with, as her lazy bastard of a husband hadn't been near her for years.

All of a sudden, I became so dizzy and felt sick in my mouth. I couldn't control it and there were no more cubicles free; I had no choice but to throw up in the sink. The two women were gobsmacked.

One of them looked at me in disgust; 'Oh my god, you've got sick on my dress. I've just bought this from Bernadette's on the precinct.'

The other was a bit more caring; 'You ok love? Had too much to drink?'

'No, I responded, it's not that.' I didn't want them to think I couldn't handle my alcohol, but I'd walked right into it.

'You pregnant love?'

I didn't answer her. I muttered an apology and went toward the door. As I did, Barbara Bentley walked in.

'Aw Chrissie, Chrissie I'm so sorry about asking you if you were up the duff before.'

'Jesus Christ,' I snapped, 'leave me the fuck alone all of you.' I steamed out of the toilets and headed back to our table just in time to witness a big fight break out.

A woman was screaming at Gill. 'You've been shagging my fuckin' husband you dirty slag. You've given him something and now he's given it to me.'

I ran over and grabbed Gill.

'Is that true?' I whispered.

'Yeah,' she said 'but, please, not here.' I burst out laughing.

I marched up to the woman and got right in her face. 'If you fucked your husband like you should have done, then he wouldn't have gone elsewhere for it, would he? Now fuck off.'

I felt a slap on the back of my head. It was my mum. 'I can't take you two fuckin' anywhere. I've had enough, get me out of here. Go on.'

She shoved us both one by one right out of the door with tears of laughter streaming down our faces. When I looked at Gill, my laughter got worse and it was starting to hurt my face.

'What did you give the husband?' I said between bouts of laughter.

'Fuck knows,' she snorted, 'but I've got a really itchy fanny.'

Again, we set off laughing. 'You're not funny either of you' mum said angrily. 'Wait until I tell your father.'

As we were walking out, one of the women who I'd almost thrown up on approached my mum.

'Excuse me love, are you leaving now?'

Mum nodded; 'Why do you ask?'

'I know it's a bit cheeky, but I don't live far from you, and I wondered if I could get a lift home?'

'Are you sure? Gene Pitney hasn't even been on yet,' asked mum.

'Yeah I've had enough,' she muttered.

'Well if you're sure, it's fine with me. Ignore these two; they've been a pair of buggers tonight,' mum said as if we were five years old. 'These are my daughters Gill and Chrissie.'

The woman looked me up and down slowly. I brushed it off; I didn't know her.

'I'm Maggie Lawrence' she said. 'Thanks for the lift.'

Chapter 18

Richard Ellis

I'd sent Maggie to The Golden Garter to get as much information on Mellor as I could, but I didn't bargain for this. It would seem that she was pregnant.

It had to be mine.

The fucking irony was that I'd had a phone call from Helen this morning letting me know that she was pregnant again. Baby number three was on its way.

I'd deal with Helen later; she wasn't going anywhere. Right now, things with Mellor were getting interesting. If she knew it was my baby, she would want to be with me. She'd be mine, just like that night she danced for me in the kitchen with lust in her eyes. Lust like I'd never seen in my life.

I spotted Peter watching me from across Maggie's living room, so I called him over. One day this kid would know I'd saved his life.

He toddled over to me with a look of awe on his face. He didn't speak much; he just looked at me like a daft hyena. Something in his eyes wasn't quite right and he was almost frothing at the mouth.

'Is he ok?' I asked Maggie.

She grunted. She clearly hadn't taken to the kid and there was possibly a bit of neglect going on. He certainly wasn't thriving. The other kids didn't like him either. At least he wasn't dead.

'What does your husband think of having the kid here?'

'My husband isn't sober long enough to notice one more kid, and if he was, he wouldn't acknowledge it anyway.'

I looked her up and down and noticed that she'd made a bit of an effort, her face was bright and she had some makeup on. It put me off. I wanted her when she was vulnerable. She shouldn't expect anything; I wasn't going to give her the power. I would have her when I wanted her.

'You look like a whore.'

'I'm your whore,' she said, in what I assumed was supposed to be a seductive voice. She was playing the fantasy game, but I didn't like it.

I slapped her across her face. 'You're just like the rest of them, a desperate piece of shit who would take your knickers off for the first bloke that came your way.'

I knew I was offending her; she hadn't had a bloke in years. I enjoyed the way she deflated in front of me; one minute, full of confidence, the next minute, feeling worthless again. Perfect. Always good to knock them down once in a while.

I looked across at little Peter who seemed to be enjoying the show even at such a young age. I think I saw a spark in his eyes somewhere; maybe he hated Maggie. I had a feeling he would be a good apprentice. I had sons, but they wouldn't amount to much, little mummy's boys that they were. Peter would be whatever I made him. He had no choice.

'Get out, you little bastard,' Maggie screamed at the kid. He stood and stared at her as though he'd taken on some confidence himself. 'Go on, fuck off,' she told him. He slowly toddled away.

'My god, are you one of those mothers who is cruel to all their children? You need to be very fucking careful, remember why he's here. It's all your doing?'

'Please, stop saying that,' she begged, 'I said something in passing to you. I never meant it.'

'You said you'd pay to have her burnt alive. People don't say that in passing Maggie,' I laughed.

'Please stop Richard, I'm sorry. I look forward to you coming over and I hate it when we don't get along.

With that, I decided to give her what she wanted. I had a hard-on anyway; might as well get some release while I was here.

I took her over the settee again. Her moans of gratefulness were well received. As I opened the cheeks of her arse with my thumbs, she sighed. She knew what was

coming and so did I.

When I finished, I noticed that Peter was watching again. He was clearly a freak; watching your mother getting fucked is not normal.

I needed to get out of this shithole. I was spending too much time here. I had better shit to do than hang about with this slut.

She must have at least seven kids including the runt. The house smelt dirty and mouldy and there was always a pile of smelly washing in the corner of the kitchen. The table was covered in pieces of cars which her pathetic husband had left lying about.

'I'm going.'

'Ok,' she muttered

And with that, I was out of there. The blue sky was slightly visible behind the greying cloud, and as I approached my car, there was a definite chill in the air.

I went to see my mother. Her house was pristine and her garden was neat with lots of flowers and plants that made it most welcoming. She would spend hours on her old knees planting shrubs and making borders. She was a proud woman.

When you walked through the door, the smell of freshly baked bread greeted you. She had two little Jack Russell dogs that yapped like fucking mad. They were her babies, and they came before anyone, even me.

I was shocked to see my cousin, Madge, sitting with my mother holding a cup and fucking saucer on her lap, pretending to be a lady.

'What are you doing here?' I asked her abruptly.

'Don't be so rude Richard,' said my mother. 'She's come to see me of course. Anyway, I could ask you the same question. Sit down and I'll make you a cup of tea.'

I did as I was told, but as soon as she went to the kitchen, I questioned Madge.

'Did you know Mellor was pregnant with my kid?'

'I don't know anything,' she protested. 'I don't want anything to do with any of this, keep me out of it.'

'So you do know something then, or there'd be nothing to keep out of?'

'I'm pregnant,' she said.

It was not what I'd expected to hear.

'To that Holland waster?' I asked her. 'How did he manage that? Did you have to go to The Lion and pull your knickers down round the back of the pub?' I laughed.

Without warning, I felt a hard slap on the back of my head. Christ! My mother was like a stealth fucking ninja or something.

'You're a disgrace Richard Ellis. How dare you speak to your cousin like that? Now apologise or get out.'

It took all my strength not to lash out at the old witch. How fucking dare she hit me? And in front of Madge too. I could have pounded her fucking face in but I wouldn't.

I had a flashback to my childhood; she made mine and my father's lives hell. She was controlling and intimidating whereas dad was weak. I watched him take so much shit from this woman. No woman would ever treat me like that; I learnt to stand up for myself. A lot of my strength came from her.

She pushed me hard which helped me with my career, and I did well at school due to the fact she'd never let me do anything normal. I had to study and I had to work. She was a bully, but some good had come out of it.

'Would you like a lift home Madge?' I offered.

'I'll walk thanks Richard,' came Madge's response.

'I only want to help; if you're pregnant, it would be easier for you to have a lift.'

My mum bought it. 'Oh let him take you love. It'll do you no harm to get a lift instead of walking all that way.'

Madge conceded. I could tell she wasn't comfortable with the idea.

'Let's finish our brew first,' I said and smiled. I always got what I wanted.

As soon as we got in my car, I pounced.

'I want to know if it's my kid.'

'Why? You're not interested in the ones you have, why

would this one be any different? And I don't appreciate what you said about Jon, he's a good man who works hard, so what if he likes a drink?'

'You've developed a fucking mouth, haven't you? Better be careful it doesn't get you in trouble,' I warned.

'I don't even speak to her anymore. You told me not to, remember? You told me to keep away and that she was a trouble causer and a liar.' She looked at me, hoping that would be enough. It wasn't.

She continued. 'I've heard nothing to confirm whether she's actually pregnant, or whether it's just gossips making something out of nothing.'

'I want it confirmed then,' I said. I stared at her so she'd understand the seriousness of what I had to say; 'I want it confirmed whether there is a kid, and whether or not it's mine.'

'Alright, I get it,' she said. 'Now let me out of this car.'

She stormed off across the estate scared and angry. I laughed as I watched her trying to maintain her composure.

I needed to know for sure. Then I would make my next move.

Chapter 19

Christine Mellor

Chris was waiting for me at our house when we got home from The Garter. We gave him the highlights from the night and he found it all very amusing. My mum was still simmering with anger, and me and Gill still found the whole thing hilarious.

'Shall we go back to ours now?' Chris asked as soon as we were alone.

'Ours?' I smiled. 'How is everyone?'

'Everyone is good.'

'Good.'

We were silent for a moment before I did what I'd been dreading.

'Chris, I need to tell you something, but I'm scared of what will happen when I do.'

'I already know,' he muttered.

'What? How?'

He shrugged; 'You know what it's like round here; something gets said and it's like bloody wildfire.'

'I'm sorry, I wanted to tell you myself. I just couldn't find a good time.'

He put his arms around me.

'I don't care. I don't care whether or not I'm the biological father. I promise I will always look after you, and if you're having a baby, then it's ours. It's our responsibility to share, and that monster will never get his hands on it. It's our baby, you're the mum and I'm the dad. End of story.'

I was immediately overwhelmed with fear, excitement and apprehension. I burst into tears, and as my sobbing was just about to get out of control, Gill came into the hall.

'Are you really pregnant Chrissie?' she asked.

'Yeah, she is,' Chris said. He was protective as always. 'It's my fault. I should have been more careful.'

'Mum will go fucking bananas you know that don't

you?' said Gill shaking her head. 'You better get off; we'll deal with it tomorrow.'

She was right. I don't' think I could muster up the strength to deal with mum without a good nights sleep.

As we lay in bed later, Chris held me tight. I was as happy as I could be considering the circumstances, and if nothing else, at least I felt safe.

The radio was playing in the background. I smiled at the sound of the DJ. His smooth voice made my eyes heavy.

Then I heard the dulcet tones of Marvin Gaye, and I was taken right back to that night.

His sly smile. The tug of the arm. The bed. The smell of piss. The struggle. The pain. Confusion, guilt, regret.

My sleep was restless. I dreamt I had a baby boy and named him Richard. When the nurse handed him to me, he had Richard Ellis's face, but his eyes were red like the devil's.

Chapter 20

Richard Ellis

I'd given my orders. I knew even though Madge had acted like an idiot, she would do what I'd asked.

I needed to know if Mellor was carrying my kid. I had every right to know. I knew once she had got her head around it being mine that she would drop Parker.

I'd move Helen out of that house in Wilmslow. Chrissie would love it there. She'd be so grateful to me.

I decided to go home to Helen. There were times I needed to be a father to the boys and show some interest in her pregnancy. Even though she wasn't in my long term plans, it was the here and now.

I took a few days off work. I worked hard and deserved to be waited on hand and foot every now and then.

As I approached the house in Wilmslow, I anticipated the scene that awaited. My beautiful wife would be there waiting for me in our beautiful home. My boys would be happy to see me. 'Hello daddy,' they would say politely — no common estate dialect from these boys. No, my boys were different. They were being brought up away from the scum that would only ruin them.

The huge gates opened, and she was walking towards the car to greet me just as I had pictured. She was an angel; there was something so innocent about her that made her look even more beautiful than she was.

My happiness was cut short.

She wasn't alone. A man was walking out of the house with her; he looked like a builder. Who the fuck was he?

She was laughing with him until she saw my face, then a look of terror took over. Why would she look so frightened if nothing was going on?

'Hi,' she smiled. 'This is Jon Holland. He's fixed the leak near the front door.' She looked uncomfortable as she introduced him to me.

Jon Holland was young and rugged, with dark skin from constantly working outdoors. His scruffy vest showed off his big, hard muscles.

I felt a twinge of something that I rarely felt. I felt insecure. I knew she found him attractive. Her body language said it all. The way she gently played with her hair, her puppy dog eyes looking at him gratefully as if he'd fixed more than the leak.

I could feel my blood starting to boil.

'Alright mate,' he said, his smile was wide. 'Nice gaff you've got here.' He nodded towards the house.

I was conscious that Madge might have told him unpleasant things about me. I didn't want him gossiping to Helen. I decided to be nice to the fucker until he was off my property. I'd make him doubt anything he'd heard about me from that council estate scum.

'Nice to meet you, Jon,' I said getting out of my car.

I put forward my hand for him to shake. I hated a weak handshake. I hated a weak man. He nearly broke my fucking hand as he shook it.

'Thanks for sorting that leak out. I'm always trying to get around to it myself, but a job like mine doesn't allow for much spare time.' I was letting him know how important I was. I had better things to do than menial household tasks.

'You're welcome mate,' he said, still smiling. His rough accent was embarrassing. He sounded thick.

'How's Madge doing?' I asked, 'Oh and congratulations,' I added politely. I turned my attention to my wife.

'Did you know they are also having a baby, Helen?' I smiled at her and could see the relief on her face; relief that I wasn't angry with her for her having another man at the fucking house.

I didn't care who came to the house, but I did care about the looks she was giving him. I wouldn't react while Holland was here, but she'd get it when he'd gone.

After more tedious small talk, he got in his old red Ford Transit van. He drove out of the huge gates and waved at Helen as he left. I noticed the little giggle she tried to hide.

I needed to put her in her place. I needed to wipe the stupid fucking grin from her face.

The boys interrupted my thoughts.

'Mum. Dad,' they shouted, running over to us. 'We've found a baby squirrel. It looks hurt. Look'. They pointed to something moving in the grass.

All I could see was red mist. I picked up the gardening fork that lay against the outhouse and stuck it right in the fucking squirrel.

'Now get in the house, all of you,' I said, my voice calm.

I looked at the three shocked faces. They were too shocked to cry. Their mother gathered her long dress, which was covered in orange, yellow and brown flowers, and grabbed her two boys as if she thought they might get it next. The stupid slut.

I walked to my car to get my bag before following them inside. The big oak door was left ajar, but there was silence in the house. I put my bag down and wandered around looking for them. I walked up the central staircase and found them all in one of the boy's bedrooms.

They were all cuddled up, crying their eyes out.

'What's up with you all?' I asked. 'Dad's home; you should all be happy, not sad.'

I beckoned to Helen to come out of the room. She came, although she was reluctant to leave the boys.

'What's up with them?' I asked.

'You've just killed a baby squirrel right in front of them.' She was sobbing.

'You've just flirted with Jon Holland right in front of me.'

Her jaw dropped. I waited for her response.

She didn't have one.

'Did he come on to you?'

She shook her head and finally found her voice.

'He came to fix the leak. It was your idea.'

'How many times has he been?'

'He came yesterday, but he forgot masking tape, so he came back to finish it off today.'

'So he's obsessed with you? I can tell by the way you were both looking at each other that something has gone on. When's he coming back?'

'Well, I asked him to do more work on the house. Richard, I'm pregnant for god sake, and so is Madge.'

'What's that got to do with anything?' I paused. 'I'll tell you what Helen,' the emphasis on her name made her wince, 'it's a good job I have my own thing going on. It's a good job I have other women to talk to, other women who care and don't fuckin' flirt with other men in front of me.'

A vision of Christine Mellor flashed before me. I pictured her dancing, sticking those tits out and putting her hands down her knickers, god she had wanted it.

'You looked like a fucking whore the way you looked at him and played with your horrible, frizzy hair.'

She touched her hair consciously.

'What do you mean, other women?' she asked. 'You always say it. There must be some truth in it.'

She was always suspicious.

'When you say other women?' she carried on. 'Do you mean one of the tramps from the estate?'

'Tramps?' I repeated. 'Do you mean those who have lives, friends, and morals. Those tramps? You're so fucking jealous of me. Jealous of my life. Jealous of the friends I have and all because you have nothing, nothing but your stupid boys who whine like girls. Your pathetic sons who you mollycoddle and wrap in cotton wool so that they cry for you constantly.'

I started pacing up and down the long hallway.

'I bet you've never given them a clout around the ear. Well, I will be doing this week.'

Her beautiful face turned ugly in front of me.

'Look at you! You're not all sweetness and light now, are you? You've got such an angry streak in you. Everyone thinks you're all sweet and innocent. If only they could see you now, dying to slap me. It's because you know I'm right, you're a fucking whore and a shit mother.'

And there it was, a sharp blast across my face.

'You will never strike my sons', she fumed.

'They'll be violent anyway with a mother like you.'

'I didn't flirt with Jon Holland,' she gritted her teeth. 'He's just a nice man.'

'A nice fucking man who gets pissed daily while Madge carries his fucking bastard child.'

I spat in her stupid face.

'Hit me again you whore, and I'll fucking kill you and that bastard inside of you, do you fucking hear me?'

She rubbed her belly as though she was protecting her unborn child. 'You wouldn't dare.'

'Try me.' I launched forward and pulled her hair so hard that she fell on the floor and as she fell, I punched her in the back of her head.

She lay there for a while as I paced up and down, adrenalin rushing through my body. I felt no remorse.

She wanted fucking attention and she got it. Now she was lying there, pretending she was hurt.

'Get up and stop being so dramatic, I hardly touched you.'

I was not sorry. The whole fucking morning had been a disaster because of her acting like a whore with Jon fucking Holland.

She had ruined my week off and I wouldn't forget it.

Chapter 21

Christine Parker

I was married.

We were Chris and Christine Parker. Mr and Mrs Parker. The Parkers.

It still hadn't quite finished sinking in.

We had our own house. We didn't own it; we rented it. We'd jumped the list because my Aunt Carol had lived there before us.

Our baby was due in a couple of weeks. It had been a difficult few months.

The difficulty had been breaking the news to my parents. They hit the roof, but Chris managed to convince them that everything would be ok and that he would look after the baby and me. Of course, dad had made us get married as if to prove it.

I was barely sixteen and lived in a three bedroomed house with a husband.

All our furniture had been donated or loaned to us. There was a big, blue three-piece suite; it looked like it was bobbly, but that was the style. We had an old double bed, and Chris's mum had sorted some bedding out for us. Gill got us a washing machine from the rag and bone man after her neighbour had said it was no good. It worked, it just needed a new plug. It was a twin tub with all the mod cons.

We didn't have a fridge, but there was a small, dark outhouse with no windows which we used for storing butter, lard and other items that needed keeping cool. We had buckets of cold water in there to keep the milk in. It was ideal. Next to it was a coal bunker and Chris had already started to collect big logs of wood for our fire, in preparation for winter. There was no way we could afford coal.

Chris's mum gave us some old curtains and insisted on hanging them for us.

'I'll hook them up here and you can move them into the

bedroom at night to keep the light out in the mornings. It'll do until we can get you another pair.'

Chris was clinging onto her as she stood on the back of the chair to put them up.

I looked down at my bump which was hidden by my one and only maternity dress. I'd got it from Gill's friend who had already had a baby. It was black with red flowers on it and it made me feel very womanly.

Chris saw me looking at my bump and gave me his warm, beautiful smile.

I thought about our wedding day. It had been fast and cheap. We couldn't get married in a church, much to my mum's annoyance. I was pregnant, and it wasn't really appropriate, so the Town Hall would have to do.

I'd manage to squeeze into mum's old wedding dress, that she swore had been too big for her on her wedding day. Chris wore a pale blue suit with the biggest collars you'd ever seen, and big, blue flares to match. He wore a purple shirt and a blue tie. He probably looked ridiculous, but to me, he looked perfect.

After we were married, we went back to my mum and dad's for beef paste sandwiches, pork pies and cake.

Dad propped a beer keg on a chair, and people drank out of small paper cups as we didn't have enough glasses.

I watched as the children of relatives pretended to be drunk. The adults laughed into the night, actually getting drunk. Everyone was having fun and I was enjoying myself. It had turned out to be a lovely day.

The party went on through the night. Dad got his records out and started playing songs from the early 60s. He made a good DJ.

Madge was there with Jon. I was glad as we were both having babies soon and I had missed her friendship.

She caught my eye through the gathering of people at my parents' house. It was getting pretty crowded in there. She was pointing to the front door as though she wanted me to go outside.

I followed her request and headed out of the front door;

people were in the garden anyway as it was a warm evening. She pointed toward the gate and mouthed the words 'The Area'. I assumed she wanted to meet me in private; maybe she had something to tell me that she didn't want Jon to hear.

'The Area' was a big square at the back of the maisonettes full of communal washing lines, where everybody in the square dried their washing. Kids would play football there, even when the washing was out. There was a wire fence surrounding it to keep out intruders because apparently, some people thought washing was worth nicking.

I bumped right into him. I couldn't breathe. It was as though he had hold of my throat, but he didn't. He pushed me up against the wall, and I wanted to cry.

'Please don't hurt me Richard,' I begged.

'Oh, I wouldn't hurt you, Chrissie Mellor.'

I wanted to correct him; my name was now Chrissie Parker, but it wasn't the time or the place.

'I'm asking you now, once and for all. Is that my fuckin' baby in there?' He slapped my stomach with his hand and it hurt.

I couldn't answer him; I was so afraid of what he might do next.

'Because if it is, I will be back for it, and you'll never see the little fucker again.' He grinned. 'Remember Kevin?'

I did remember Kevin, but by now I was shaking and feeling very faint. I passed out.

The next thing I remember is the blue lights of the ambulance and a crowd around me.

The ambulance man confirmed that I was ok, and I'd just fainted.

The party was over. People felt it inappropriate to dance and sing, and dad had switched off the record player.

'I'm ok, honestly.'

I half wanted everyone to be as they were and carry on enjoying themselves.

'Come on Mrs Parker,' said Chris. 'Let's get you home.'

As we got to the front door of our new house, my new husband picked me up and carried me over the threshold.

I lay in bed that night, my wedding night, thinking about Richard Ellis and wondering if Madge had known he was there and why she'd helped him.

Chapter 22

Richard Ellis

I'd been keeping away from Helen since my last visit. After all, it hadn't been the pleasant experience I had expected. It started with her acting like a whore around that wanker, Jon Holland. Not only that, she'd been violent towards me. Her behaviour had not improved throughout the week. She constantly came to complain to me about her feelings.

I had things to do at night which didn't involve her, but she couldn't accept it. She wasn't happy about going to bed alone every night and then being left alone in the day while I rested.

She'd say she felt a million miles from me. I didn't have time to placate her. I was a busy man.

'You need to sleep and rest,' I'd say, letting her think that this was for her benefit.

Weak, pathetic woman. I was quickly losing respect for Helen and decided to stay away.

Then I got a call saying she had been taken sick. I would have to go; I couldn't just ignore the fact that she was unwell.

I drove to the house with dread. The last thing I needed right now was a hormonal woman losing her kid.

When I arrived, her Aunt Doreen was with her. That's all I needed; interfering old witch.

Helen was leaning over the kitchen table looking like she was in a lot of pain.

'What's up?' I demanded.

She didn't even try to respond. Doreen explained that Helen was having pain at the top of her legs and was finding it difficult to walk.

'Then sit down,' I suggested. Surely that made more sense than to try and walk about. I felt exasperated.

I helped her across to the living room with her clinging to me as if her life depended on it. I guided her to the leather

Chesterfield sofa.

'Come on baby,' I whispered in her ear, 'it's going to be ok.' She looked unsure. She clearly wasn't going to forget what had happened last time in a hurry.

I would make her forget.

'Doreen, put the kettle on and make Helen and I a cup of tea,' I ordered. 'Boys, go upstairs please; good lads.'

Helen looked on edge.

'I can be nice, you know.' I gave her my best smile.

She smiled back. 'I know. Thank you.'

'Have you seen the doctor?' I asked her.

'No, I was going to wait and see how I felt tomorrow.'

'Are you sure?'

'Yeah, the pain has eased off a bit.'

'Come on,' I held her close to me. 'It's all going to be ok; you know that, don't you? 'I'm here now.'

I told her how beautiful she was. She really was. Her vulnerability made her look like an angel.

The next few days, I looked after her. We ate together and bathed together. Most importantly I let her fall asleep in my arms every evening. We'd lie in bed together, and I'd stroke her hair until she slept.

She was delicate, but she wasn't against giving me the odd blow job. I had made it perfect.

I spent time engaging with the boys too, and Helen flourished. Her mood improved, and she was sweetness and light again.

The hard work was worth it, but it meant I'd lost touch with what was going on elsewhere. I needed to get back to work and back to normality.

Most people would be content with the beautiful wife, loving children and a luxurious home, but I needed something else.

The lack of destruction and control was causing me to feel uneasy and isolated. Every so often, I'd get a knot in my stomach. I'd feel sick and shaky and fearful. I couldn't relax. I needed destruction; it gave me a sense of control. I had to get away.

There was somebody else out there; somebody who was having my baby; somebody pretending to be happy. I couldn't let her and that dick, Parker, live happily ever after with my baby.

I knew Helen wouldn't be happy when I told her that I was going.

'When?' she asked.

'Now.'

'Please don't go,' she almost begged. 'It's been so good you being here. The boys will miss you.'

Fucking bitch, making me feel bad. She was good at this. She sidled up to me on the couch.

'You've had a nice time, haven't you?'

She was starting to make my blood boil.

'Nice time? Is that how you define a nice time?' I was fuming. 'I've looked after your stupid boys because you made yourself ill and coerced me into coming when you knew I was busy. I made you better just by being here, which proves there was nothing wrong with you. You just wanted some attention.'

She looked calm. 'Ok,' she said.

I cooled down a little. She clearly wanted to avoid an argument. She was learning.

'I'm going to get my bag. Make sure you take the telephone upstairs and I'll ring you later.

'Ok.'

I collected my things and returned to kiss her goodbye.

'Right, I'm off, see you later.'

'Ok,' she repeated.

I walked to my car and dropped my bag in the boot. I was about to drive off, but something wasn't right.

She had been far to calm. 'Ok,' she'd said. There were no emotional goodbyes, no begging for me to stay. She wasn't upset that I was leaving and I think I knew why.

Jon Holland. I bet he was coming over for a fuck. The bastards probably had it all arranged. She probably couldn't wait for me to leave so she could whore it up with that scruffy wanker.

I marched back into the house. She was crying.

'You've arranged for Holland to come over, haven't you? That's why you couldn't wait to get rid of me.'

She didn't respond.

'Tell me,' I yelled. The boys stopped what they were doing and watched intently. The little twats were about to get a show.

I slapped Helen around the head. 'Why can't you look at me?' I yelled. 'You're a fucking con artist. I put people like you in prison every day.'

The boys started crying.

'Look Helen, you've upset your two little girls,' I sneered.

I was fuming; she was no better than any of the scum on the estate

'You're just like the rest of them. I'm going, and I won't be back no matter what you pretend to have wrong with you.'

'Please, Richard,' she said, pleading with me. 'I don't want to fight. I'm nearing the end and I don't have any energy. I need to lie down.'

She headed toward the oak staircase.

'You've done fuck all, all week. You should be full of energy,' I shouted.

I wanted to drag her down the stairs by her hair, and I know that half of her wanted me to do that. She was sick in the head. This pregnancy was making her selfish, and she was bringing me down. I wasn't going to let her.

I left the boys standing there crying. She could do what the fuck she wanted. I was done with them all.

Chapter 23

Christine Parker

I'd done my last shift at work, but I'd be going back once I'd had the baby. We couldn't afford for me not to.

The girls had made such a fuss; the older women had knitted me cardigans, coats, blankets and little hats all in lemon and green. They'd bought me some nappies and safety pins. I laughed at the time and said I was sure I'd never get the knack of putting on a baby's nappy. I still couldn't quite believe I was having a baby.

It was getting difficult to move now. I felt like a big whale, but Chris was being a wonderful husband, looking after me and making sure I had everything I needed.

He never left for work in the morning without lighting the oven in the kitchen so that the house was warm when I got up. He'd leave a hot cup of tea next to my bed and would never fail to kiss me goodbye before he left. He was gentle when we had sex, careful not to hurt me, but he could still thrill me to the core.

He helped me get in and out of the bath and we'd laugh because I think he struggled more than I did.

He worked hard to make our home nice.

All the while, we both knew that this wasn't his baby, but we would never say it out loud.

I was meeting Madge today. She had asked to see me. I didn't know why but it wouldn't do any harm to find out.

Christmas had been and gone, and the weather was awful now. The estate glistened, white with snow. I just hoped that I didn't fall flat on my arse as I'd never be able to get myself back up again.

I walked up the long road to The Lion where I was meeting Madge. The trees on either side looked cold and naked, nothing to keep them warm as they swayed with the weight of the snow on their boughs.

The new orange buses that had just been introduced in

Manchester were doing their best to plough through the snow, turning it into black mush.

Children were sliding down the white slopes on orange bread trays that they'd nicked from the back of the shops. It was warming to hear their laughter and made me smile as I trudged to the pub.

I was always conscious when walking alone and constantly checked behind me and over the road. I'd not heard anything about Richard Ellis for a while. Hopefully, the bastard had fallen down a snow hole. I prayed that I'd seen the last of him, but I knew it was unlikely.

I was sure the constant ringing of my mum and dad's phone in the middle of the night was down to him. The smashed windows at Chris's parent's house were probably his doing as well.

I looked down at my huge bump; I hoped it was a girl. The dream about having a baby Richard with red eyes was enough to put me off having a boy.

The pub was packed. There were a handful of small round tables with stools to match. Each table had a huge ashtray on it, which George would have to empty constantly throughout the day. Local men who didn't work anymore congregated here in their blazer jackets and flat caps. It would soon be getting dark.

The coal fire roared in the corner and the dark, orangey glow made me feel warm. I took off my red wool coat. It had been my mum's when she was pregnant with me; luckily, she never threw anything away.

I spotted Madge waiting for me. I looked around suspiciously just in case he was waiting in the shadows.

The landlady, Lizzie, who was probably not much older than me, shouted her greeting as I walked past the bar.

'Alright love, colder than our Georges heart out there, isn't it?'

I laughed. She was referring to her husband, the landlord, who was a grumpy sod. They had a beautiful little boy Tommy, who would come down and mingle with the customers.

'Alright Lizzie?' I responded with a smile.

Madge was smiling as I tried to squeeze past the tables to get to where she was.

I laughed when I got there. 'Jesus! If I'd have turned the wrong way, I'd have been lodged between those two tables.'

'Me too.' She giggled and pointed to her perfect bump.

'You're not even that big' I complained. She was nowhere near as big as me.

'Where's Jon?' I asked.

'Don't know. He'll be here in a bit, I'm sure. The weather is just slowing everyone down.'

Lizzie's voice interrupted our conversation.

'Can I help you love?' she shouted towards the door letting the whole pub know a stranger had just walked in.

I looked across the smoky room at the new arrival. She looked like an angel; a dark angel, sad and desperate. She looked around, catching sight of Madge and me. She pointed towards us and headed on over to where we sat.

She looked like a dark angel. I'm sure there was a glow around her.

'Who's that?' I asked Madge.

She walked towards me, and I noticed a perfectly formed baby bump under her expensive looking poncho. My stomach tightened as she reached us.

She pointed to my stomach. 'I think that's my husband's baby,' she said. Her tone was so matter of fact. There was no hint of aggression or threat. If anything, she looked nervous.

I tried to answer, but the pains in my stomach forced me to double over momentarily.

'Did you tell her I was going to be here?' I leant over and asked Madge through gritted teeth.

'No, honestly Chrissie.'

'Then why did you want to see me?'

I never did find out.

Without warning, there was a gush of water on the floor. I thought my waters had broken which baffled me as I hadn't felt a thing. I quickly realised it was her, the dark angel. She stood there in stunned silence, looking at me and then the floor as if needing an explanation.

I stood up, and as I did, my waters broke too.

The next few hours passed in a blur. I felt like I had been lifted from my body and plonked on the side to watch. None of what was happening felt real.

The ambulances arrived, and before I knew it, I was being wheeled along shiny hospital corridors. I wanted Chris.

'Has anybody managed to get hold of my husband?' I asked the nurse who was pushing me. She wore a lilac uniform with a white apron and hat; her face was stern as she shook her head.

As we turned a corner, I spotted another pregnant woman. It was the dark angel from the pub. She looked right at me. It was not a look of hostility as I'd expected, but a look of deep sadness and desperation. Her eyes were so red that she looked as though she had been crying for weeks. She looked like a woman who'd lost hope.

I reached out to touch her hand and she did the same. She barely brushed my skin, but the spark of electricity that ran through my body was unbelievable. She leant over to speak, but her face was suddenly overcome with a look of fear. I knew instantly that Richard was there.

The nurse wheeled me away, but not before I caught sight of him marching towards her. He looked furious.

He leant down carefully towards her face and whispered something. Her reaction made my belly turn over.

Tears rolled down her face; tears of frustration, tears of fear, tears of helplessness.

I felt as though I could feel exactly what she was feeling, as though I was somehow connected to her pain. Perhaps childbirth makes you hypersensitive to the emotions of others; I don't know. All I know is that I felt a strange bond. I wanted to help her, but the pain of my labour prevented me.

'Quick,' I shouted to the nurse, 'I think I need to push.'

I was scared. 'Where's Chris?' I yelled to anybody that could hear me.

I was pushed into a room where I was given gas and air as a midwife helped me change into a hospital gown.

He was there, in the room.

'I want him to leave,' I said out loud. 'I want my husband.'

Richard was asked to leave the room. It wasn't the done thing for a man to be in the room with you while you gave birth anyway.

I desperately wanted Chris.

I was helped back on the bed. I was going to have my baby and I was going to have it soon.

I started to push; my god, I pushed. The pain was unbearable. I stayed calm; I breathed deeply, just as mum had told me to.

My brow was covered with sweat; my breathing was fast and furious. The pain was so constant; I couldn't tell if it was getting better or worse.

I let out an almighty scream and pushed as hard as I could. I pushed the night of the rape away; I pushed the thought out of my mind and concentrated on the life I was bringing into the world.

'It's a girl!' The midwife was delighted and so was I.

While the midwives were still checking everything was ok with me and my baby daughter, Mum, Gill and Chris arrived.

I started sobbing. I sobbed for me and I sobbed for the dark angel.

'Come on now love, what's up?' My mum said softly. She was the most cheerful I'd ever seen her in my life.

Chris kissed my face. 'She's beautiful; she has your dark hair and beautiful blue eyes.'

With that, she let off the loudest scream you have ever heard in your life.

Mum and Gill went to get a cup of tea, leaving Chris and me alone.

'His wife came to the pub for me,' I whispered, 'she

looks so sad.'

Chris was about to respond when the door opened, and Richard Ellis appeared. He was like a bad smell that just wouldn't go away.

'Ok Parker, you take my daughter for now, but you just wait until you have a daughter of your own. I'll take her like I took her mother. You can count on that.'

Before Chris was out of his chair, the coward had slithered away like the snake he was.

'Leave it Chris,' I said. 'Please. The bad will out. I really believe he'll get what he deserves someday soon. We have a beautiful baby girl. Forget about him.'

Chris looked torn, but his face softened as he looked at our daughter. She was so innocent, so beautiful.

'Can we call her Pamela?' Chris asked. I wasn't keen on the name, but I wanted it to be his choice. I at least wanted to give him that.

'Ok,' I agreed, 'we can call her Ella for short.' He grinned from ear to ear, and Ella Parker she would be.

Chapter 24

Chris Parker: Five years later

The years flew by, and I couldn't believe my baby was already a feisty five-year-old. I'd had a second baby, Henry, who was the spitting image of his dad and I was pregnant with our third child. Chris and I were never bored that's for sure.

We didn't have much, but I was happy. My husband was the best dad ever and doted on both our children, treating Ella as if she were his own.

We managed to keep them warm and fed and that was all that mattered. They were loved unconditionally, especially my Ella.

I'd never be able to forget that awful night, but I had to admit, some good actually did come out of it. If I had to relive the nightmare again, knowing she'd be there at the end of it, then I would.

There was no doubt she was his. I could see his distinctive good looks, and when she asserted herself, I could see his confidence.

Her father was a dangerous man, a thief who hadn't thought twice about stealing my virginity. I had no doubt he would kill anyone who got in his way. I shuddered at the thought of the fire that had killed Janet and her baby. I was sure he was responsible; I couldn't shake the thought that he'd meant for Chris and me to die that night.

Try as I might to forget him, he was never out of my thoughts for long.

I often wondered if I should have reported him to the police for raping me, but I knew it would have done no good. Richard Ellis was the police. He'd already shown us what a dangerous man he was, and I wanted to keep him as far away from my family as possible.

Chris and I agreed to never talk about him, but that wasn't easy where we lived. He always seemed to worm his way in, one way or another.

'I called at your mum's earlier and Lil Thomson was there,' Chris told me one night.

Lil was my mum and dad's neighbour and the biggest gossip I had ever met. She was like the bloody News of the World and what she didn't know wasn't worth knowing.

'What did she say?' I asked

'She said Maggie Lawrence's kid is always with Richard Ellis. It doesn't make sense to me.'

It didn't to me either. Nobody had ever seen Richard Ellis with his own kids, why would he spend so much time with someone else's.

The kid was called Peter, and he was a bit of an oddball. There was definitely something not right about the poor lad. He looked like he'd had a trauma that he'd never quite recovered from. It was certainly bizarre that Richard Ellis would take an interest in him.

It was well-known that Richard had been a regular visitor of Maggie. It had crossed my mind that Peter could be Richard's kid, but it didn't add up. Looking at him, you could clearly see he had the Irish looks of his dad and other siblings. He looked nothing at all like Ellis.

Maggie Lawrence had disappeared off the face of the earth. The police had investigated about as hard as they investigated the fire at Janet's. They didn't care much about anyone on the estate; the less of us there was, the better.

Her pathetic husband was left to look after the kids. She took her daughters with her, but the lads stayed with old man Lawrence. One by one they were removed for various reasons, except Peter.

I wondered if Richard was in some way responsible. I wouldn't put it past him.

Maggie Lawrence had lived next door to Madge and Jon Holland. According to the gossips, Richard had helped them get the house.

'How did that Madge Holland get that big three-bedroom house?' people would ask.

I missed Madge's friendship, but I had decided it was

better to do everything I could to keep Richard out of our lives. I couldn't ignore the fact that Madge was his cousin.

She and Jon Holland had also had a baby girl. I heard they'd named her Elizabeth and she was well and thriving, unlike their marriage. Jon spent every hour he wasn't working in The Lion while Madge brought up Elizabeth almost single-handedly.

It was common knowledge that she'd had enough. She had never really belonged around here and wouldn't be able to deal with the likes of Jon Holland. He might have been a grafter, but he was also a boozer; she couldn't compete.

'Mum, Mum,' Ella shouted, interrupting my thoughts.

It was as though there was an emergency every time that kid wanted me.

'What's up?' I asked.

'Can Nessa come in to play?'

Vanessa Brown was five years old and always playing out on her own. The poor kid looked like she could do with a good bath and a brush running through her hair.

Last time she came to play, Ella got headlice; I couldn't be arsed picking the little fuckers out again.

Too late. Nessa was standing at the front door with Ella; her long auburn hair was a mass of lugs and knots. If she was going to give Ella lice again, she probably already had.

'Mum said I could come and play at yours,' said Nessa. She had a shy look to her. She was a quiet little girl, but then again, next to Ella, anyone would seem quiet.

'Did she now?' I smiled. It wasn't her fault her mother wanted her out of the way for an hour and I'd rather have them in here than playing out in the cold.

'Ok Ella. You can both play in your bedroom if you take our Henry with you. Just don't bloody mess it up, I've tidied that room twenty times today.'

She scrunched her little nose up and answered me back as she always did.

'You've not tidied it up twenty times; you've been gabbing with Aunty Gill.'

'Go on, you cheeky little madam,' I laughed.

And off they ran up the stairs, Nessa carrying Henry like he was her own, his mass of blonde curls making his face look tiny.

I made him a bottle of tea and took it up to them.

'How's your mum and dad,' I asked the little girl. I was only being nosey. They were a big family who lived in a four-bedroomed house off the main road that ran through the estate.

'They're ok,' she smiled. She looked at me with big brown eyes and the longest eyelashes you've ever seen. She looked all sweet and innocent, and she really was.

Nessa's parents were probably the same age as my parents. Rumour had it that her dad was a nonce and that wasn't good round our way. I didn't even want to think about Ella going to that house. I didn't want to think about Ella being out of my sight. She had recently started school and that was bad enough.

I carried on with my day, my third baby fluttering away happily inside me.

As I was walking down the stairs, I saw a brown envelope on the doormat. The postman had already been so I had no idea what it might be. I picked it up and took it through to the kitchen.

It was addressed to Christine Parker, and the writing was especially nice. Who did I know with writing that fancy? A sudden thought hit me, and my stomach turned.

Before I had chance to open the envelope, I heard Chris coming in. I quickly shoved the letter into my big shopping bag that hung by the back door.

'Do you want a brew?' I asked as I filled up the little kettle that permanently sat on the gas stove.

'Aye, go on, thanks love.'

We got chatting and the time flew by. The three kids came down the stairs hungry and thirsty, and I couldn't believe little Nessa Brown was still here.

'Jesus! Chris, you'd better take her home. Her mum and dad will be worried sick. She's been here hours.'

'Can I come dad?' Ella didn't like to be left out.

'Come on then.'

As soon as he was out the door, I retrieved the envelope from my bag and tore it open.

'Christine

I'm sorry to contact you out of the blue, but I can't stop thinking about you.

I want you to know I'm sorry I worried you; I meant no harm.

I was in real trouble after I approached you in the pub. I don't know what I was thinking, coming to find you like that but I know what a terrible thing he did, and I needed to meet you. I know what he did to you, and I'm sorry.

I have also suffered at his hands. Maybe not in the same way as you, but life is not good with him. I try to put on a brave face for my children, but it's hard to stay positive.

Anyway, I just needed to let you know why I came that day, the day our children were born. Maybe I'm crazy, but I felt as though we had a connection in the hospital and just for a moment, I felt a glimmer of hope.

I hope you will forgive me for this intrusion, but I have nobody else and nowhere to turn.

Helen Ellis

I was shaking. Was Richard behind this? My god, of course he was. It was just another one of his mind games. I screwed the letter up and threw it back in the bag.

That night I lay awake; my mind was in turmoil. Was Helen reaching out for help or was Richard messing with me? The hardest part was keeping it from Chris. I don't know how he would react, and I hadn't decided what to do yet.

'Mum! Muuuuum!' Ella was shouting for me.

I ran to her room.

'What's wrong?'

'I had a bad dream,' she said sleepily.

I crawled into bed and held my daughter tight.

As I snuggled up to my little girl, her hand brushed against mine, and I got a flashback to the night I was in labour. Helen's hand had brushed against mine just like that, and I had felt a connection too. In that moment, I knew Helen did need me; she needed my help.

Part Two

Chapter 1

Helen Ellis: 1980s

I looked around at my existence.

On paper, we were the perfect family. My husband was handsome and had a high-paying job. My sons were educated at the best schools, and each of them was dark and handsome. We had a very beautiful home, left to me by my loving parents, and plenty of money for anything we needed.

Everything appeared perfect; I had a life of luxury.

I thought about my parents often; they were taken away from me far too soon. I had a wonderful childhood, my mother doted on me, and I was my father's angel.

My paternal grandfather had been a black soldier who'd met my grandmother during World War II. My dad used to sit me on his knee and tell their story. My grandmother worked as a nurse, taking care of the injured soldiers. My grandfather, William, had been sent over from America. They fell in love but never married. Sadly, my grandfather was killed in service, and shortly after, my grandmother realised she was pregnant with my father.

My dad was a handsome man; his dark skin had the most beautiful glow. He had chocolate brown eyes and cut his afro short. He did well in his career considering black people were still treated as outcasts when he was alive.

My parents met at work. They both served in the police force and worked extremely hard to make sure I had a comfortable life.

My mother was a white woman; she used to tell me about what a hard time she'd had because of her decision to marry someone who had different coloured skin. Her father had disowned her, calling her names that she would never repeat to me. But my dad was a gentleman, and my mother never regretted her choice of husband.

I was so fortunate to have two strong, hard-working and

loving parents.

Then, one day, they were just gone, taken away from me; their words of love and wisdom went with them.

I was just a teenager and suddenly felt very alone in the world. I was distraught. That's when Richard stepped in to save me, or so I thought at the time.

I had never seen him before my parent's funeral. He'd made sure he was right by my side, and he made me feel safe and protected.

He came back to the house afterwards, as did a few others; my Aunt Doreen had made tea and sandwiches for everyone. Richard had stayed behind after everyone else left and sat down with me and Aunt Doreen. He told us that my father had asked him to look after me if anything should happen to him.

I was shocked that dad would ask anybody to look after me, let alone a stranger. Despite my initial confusion, he had paperwork to back it up; there was some legal arrangement between my father and him.

The next few years were full of mixed emotions. Richard never stayed for long; his attention was drip fed to me. I was still very much a child and I missed my parents, so when he was around, he was my lifeline.

His subtle sexual advances made me feel very uncomfortable at first, but when they stopped, I realised I missed them. He seemed to put me on a pedestal and his adoration for me was beyond belief. I loved to be near him as much as I dreaded it. Either through grief or naivety, I didn't understand that his predatory and controlling nature was wrong.

I looked around my huge living room and thought how sad it was that my once beautiful childhood home now felt like a prison. He'd even put bars on the window which he claimed was for my protection, but I knew it was for his. He had never wanted me to mix with the outside world, and the one time I'd tried, I had certainly paid for it.

What Richard didn't know was that I knew about every move he made. I had discovered his journal where he recorded everything he did; every woman he slept with, every bribe he took, every favour he was owed and every favour he called in.

At the time I'd felt totally destroyed; I was pregnant with young Richard and I was an emotional wreck. Although I was upset, I wasn't entirely surprised by what I'd read. He could be a nasty, controlling man. I know he didn't love me in a normal way because no person who loved you would be so vicious toward you.

When I'd found the journal, I sat for hours putting together pieces of his broken erratic lifestyle. Although I wasn't the only woman in his life, I did find some comfort in knowing that I was the main one; I was his wife and mother to his children.

Reading about his sexual encounters was difficult, but I gradually saw that it wasn't about the sex itself; it was about control and destruction. My husband was clearly a very sick individual and a highly dangerous person.

He didn't use the word rape in his journal, but the way he described his relationship with Christine Mellor had been disturbing. He wrote in detail about how she struggled, how she tried to push him off, begging him to stop. What sickened me the most was that he hid in the bushes waiting for her, pouncing on her like some predatory beast. I can only imagine what that poor girl must have gone through that night at the hands of my husband.

It was clear from his description that the sex with Christine had not been consensual. Despite this, he was convinced that she wanted him to do those things to her. He was deluded. He wrote about how she was obsessed with him, but it seemed to me that it was the other way around. He was following her, waiting for her at work, tormenting her at every opportunity. He was the one who was obsessed with her.

I couldn't help feeling slightly jealous. I wondered what was so wrong with me that he needed other women and why he didn't obsess about me the way he did Christine. I felt ashamed of myself for having these thoughts. What sort of person was I to be jealous of a girl who'd been viciously raped?

I thought about Christine a lot over the years. I thought about how I'd gone to find her, how we'd given birth to our children on the same night. Our children who were brother and sister that had never met; neither child was aware of their half-sibling.

Most of all I thought about the way she reached out to me and the look of pity in her eyes as our hands touched. For a moment, just a moment, I'd felt some hope. I sometimes fantasised that we were friends and that she helped me escape my husband; we were both free from his control.

I'd written to her years later, but I never received anything back. Why would I? She probably didn't trust the source, I know I wouldn't. Even if she did, why would she want contact with a rapist's wife? I just hoped that deep down she knew that I never meant her harm.

The boys were due back from school at any time, so I started to prepare their dinner. They were my life and I enjoyed cooking for them and having them nearby. They'd soon be gone if their father had his way. He'd threatened boarding school on many occasions. I'd manage to prevent it so far, but if he was serious, he'd make it happen.

My boys were my reason for breathing. They kept me going in my darkest moments.

Beautiful Robert was thirteen and looked so much like my father. He was soft and gentle and kind. David was twelve and looked almost like a male version of me. His skin tone was dark and his hair black and curly, just like mine. Richard, who was ten, was named by his father, another example of his arrogance. Young Richard was just like his dad. If I had not been awake when I'd given birth to him, I would question if he was actually mine. His mannerisms, his confidence, his blue eyes, the way his hair never looked ruffled; he was exactly like his father.

After dinner, we went for a walk. We lived in an area that was full of wildlife and trees. The River Bollin ran merrily through part of our garden. My parents had built the house themselves after buying the land from an old farmer.

While my boys ran ahead of me, I walked and thought. Life was difficult for me. I never had any adult contact except for Richard. Aunt Doreen visited occasionally, but I'm sure that was on Richard's orders and not of her own free will.

At first, Richard had been wonderful. He'd made me feel safe and loved. His temper rarely made an appearance. These days, that loving Richard was nowhere to be seen. Now I felt lucky if he spent time at the house without becoming violent or upsetting one of our sons.

I was so lost in thought that I'd lost track of time. I'd also not paid attention to where we were going; I just followed my boys.

It had started to get dark, and we'd walked for miles. The boys were coming back toward me.

'We've never been here have we mum?'

I looked around and felt slightly concerned. I'd been so wrapped up in thought that I'd not been aware of just how far we'd gone.

I looked around to get my bearings but couldn't work out where we were. Who the hell could get lost in their own garden?

The boys ran into the nearby trees, enjoying the adventure we'd accidentally embarked on.

'Boys,' I shouted, 'come back please.'

Robert and David came running out immediately.

'Where's Richard?' I panicked. 'Richard?' I shouted.

I grabbed Robert and David by the hand and walked them into the wood. It was dark, and I could barely see a thing in the poor light. Then I heard barking, lots of barking.

The three of us froze to the spot, as something ran toward us. It was Richard; he was crying and wailing.

'Run,' he yelled; 'there's dogs in there.'

We didn't have to be told twice and ran back the way we came in. The barking got further away and I was confident the dogs weren't giving chase. Perhaps they were chained up.

Chained up where? I asked myself.

We stopped running. 'Everyone ok?' I asked my boys.

Richard looked at me seriously. 'There was a house in the woods with lots of dogs; I thought they were going to get me.'

Somewhere in the back of my mind, something clicked, like a light switch being turned on. I didn't quite know what I was remembering; I couldn't quite recall the memory. Was there a house in the wood? Had I been there in my younger years? Surely, I'd remember a house. Maybe Richard had imagined it in his excitement.

We continued walking and eventually, I recognised the landscape. As we neared our house, I saw headlights coming up the dirt track. He was here.

My day just got so much worse.

He'd be livid that I wasn't there to open the gates. He used to call to let me know he was coming but not anymore. Now he'd just turn up out of the blue at different times of day. It was almost as if he was trying to catch me out.

I thought about what had just happened and felt a heat rush through my body. I felt like I couldn't breathe. I had to stand still for a minute and get myself together. I was dreading the boys telling him about our walk, dreading the questioning, dreading the accusations, dreading him.

There was no escaping it; I would have to face him. Taking a deep breath, I walked as quickly as I could to go and greet my husband.

His reaction was just as I expected. As he threw plates and pans across my beautiful kitchen, I shook my head and absorbed the absolute vile nonsense that was coming out of his mouth.

'If you ever go near that place again, I will kill you and I mean it. Who will look after the boys then? I certainly won't.'

I hated him and wondered how long I could live this way without killing him.

Chapter 2

Madge Holland

I stirred as I heard the loud barking of dogs and I was sure I could hear voices in the distance. I sat completely still, but the sound of my breathing was deafening. I needed to listen. The dogs stopped barking; I couldn't hear anything unusual. I wondered if I had imagined it, but I knew I hadn't.

I looked around the room. It was a small room with white paint peeling off the walls. Every time I woke up, there would be a split second where I'd expect to wake up in my bedroom. Then reality would hit me all over again, and I'd remember the hopeless situation I was in.

I slept on a mattress on a stone-cold floor. The blankets I'd been given to keep me warm were constantly damp from the cold.

There was one window in the room. It was too high for me to see out of and too small for me to climb out of, but it let me know if it was night or day.

This room had been my prison for the last five years. I hoped every day that one day, I would get home to my beautiful little girl, Elizabeth. I had nothing left but hope and I clung to it daily. In the early days, I'd cried every time I thought about Elizabeth, Bess, my baby. My heart ached at the idea of her thinking I'd abandoned her. I wondered now if she even remembered me. Did she hate me for leaving her?

I went through the events that had brought me here. I re-lived them every day, over and over, and each time I'd play out a different ending. The ending was never this. The ending was me living happily with Jon and Bess.

****

The night Jon came home and pissed on the settee for the second time that week was the night I finally decided that

I'd had enough.

I loved him and Bess doted on him, but I needed to get out. I decided to take Bess and go and stay with my aunt who I'd lived with before marrying Jon.

I sat Bess down and looked into her little blue eyes. I moved a blonde curl away from them so that she could see me better. I explained we were going away for a few days, but that I had an errand to run first so I would be coming back for her in the morning. She wasn't worried by this, probably because Jon's mum had come to see her and she was happy to be with her grandma. She gave me a kiss and carried on doing what she was doing.

I packed a bag for myself and one for Bess. I took mine but I still needed to grab a few essentials for Bess, so I left hers there. I walked across the green to my aunt's car which she'd kindly let me borrow.

The boy from next door was lying down on the green and playing with the grass. That kid was always in a world of his own. God knew where his mother was. I didn't ask. It was best if I didn't ask.

He looked up at me, and for the first time, I saw his face properly. He looked so familiar, and I suddenly had a realisation. I knew who little Peter Lawrence was. I knelt down to take a closer look. He stared at me intently. I recognised his Irish green eyes and his thick long lashes; there was no mistaking it.

Christ! It was baby Kevin.

As far as I knew, everybody in the Parker family thought that baby Kevin was dead; yet, here he was in full view, playing on the grass.

My mind raced. Why did Maggie Lawrence have baby Kevin? Had she taken him from the fire? I doubted it. Why would she take him and then abandon him?

My cousin, Richard, had always had an interest in Peter. He'd continued to visit him even after Maggie had disappeared. Nobody understood why, but I think I was starting to. Could it be that Richard had taken him from Janet's and left him with the Lawrences? Had he started the fire?

It made no sense, but then again, it made perfect sense. I knew that Richard was an evil man and I knew he had an obsession with Chrissie. Something had gone on that night at Janet's flat. Maybe he'd killed Janet to get to Chrissie and Chris. He hated the fact that they were together.

He was a vengeful man, no doubt, but was he capable of murder and kidnap? I thought so, and he was certainly capable of covering it up.

Shit!

I walked towards the car and put my bag in the boot. I needed to go to the chemist up the road and then make some arrangements for Bess and me so that everything was ready for us to leave tomorrow. This thing with Kevin would have to wait for now.

I closed the boot of the car and turned around. Christine Parker was standing behind me. She looked awkward.

'If you see Helen Ellis, give her this?' she said, and then stared me dead in the eye as she thrust an envelope into my hand. 'I'm trusting you.'

She walked off, and I was left holding a brown envelope with 'Helen' scrawled in pencil on the front.

I watched her as she stomped off down the road. She was pregnant again and wore her old red coat. She'd had that coat for years now. It wafted in the wind because she hadn't fastened it, perhaps the buttons had finally fallen off.

I wanted to run after her or shout her and tell her about baby Kevin. Her husband's nephew was right there in front of her on the grass and she barely glanced at him as she walked by.

The wind blew slightly and caught the envelope. I thought about what she had said; 'I'm trusting you.' What she meant was 'don't let Richard know'.

I wondered why she was writing Helen Ellis a letter. It was obviously important to her if she was taking the risk to get it to her. Richard would hit the roof if he found out.

I knew Richard would be at work and that it wouldn't take me long to drive to Wilmslow. Jon pointed out their house every time we drove by, so I knew where they lived. It was very secluded and hidden away, but I was sure I could find it.

Their home was magnificent. Richard wanted everyone to think he'd bought it, a sign of his success, but the whole world knew that Helen's parents had built it using their hard-earned cash. He wasn't fooling anyone.

As I approached the huge iron gates, I was alarmed to see a car in front of me. I quickly realised it was Richard. What was he doing here?

'It's ok,' I told myself. I'd say I was here to see him. I'd say I needed his help getting Bess and me somewhere else to live.

I stopped my car and waited. He could see me; he had probably seen me before I saw him. I could see the intensity of his blue eyes in the mirror of his car.

This was a bad idea. The last thing I wanted was a confrontation with Richard Ellis. I slammed the car into reverse; I needed to get back...

****

My thoughts were broken by a noise outside.

I'd prepare myself mentally every day just in case he turned up. He came every couple of weeks to bring me provisions. He'd given me a little stove and a kettle so I could at least have hot meals and drinks. I'd have to ration carefully though as I never knew when he'd return.

He stood in the doorway and stared at me. I tried to weigh up his mood as my next few hours would be dependent on it. I could tell he was angry about something.

'They nearly found the house,' he said, more to himself than to me.

'Who?' I asked. I felt hopeful. Maybe someone would find me.

He stroked his chin and looked at me with his intense blue eyes, but he didn't reply.

'It doesn't matter. The dogs scared them off. Don't think

for a minute that this place isn't being watched. If you try anything, I'll kill your little Bess right in front of you.

I stayed calm. 'I won't try anything,' I said. There was nothing else worth trying anyway.

'Have you seen her? My Bess?' I asked him in my nicest voice; anything he told me would give me the strength to go on.

'She goes to the local school with all the other riffraff,' he grinned. 'Her and Ella are close. Well, I suppose they are cousins, aren't they?'

I knew the circumstances of Ella's conception; he knew it made me uncomfortable.

'They're friends with the youngest Brown girl. You know the one whose father is the local nonce. I heard that while Jon props up the bar in The Lion, Bess has been staying over at the Browns.'

My heartbeat got faster. The thought of some pervert touching my little girl while Jon got pissed was unbearable.

'Don't worry,' he said. I've had them removed and taken into foster care.'

'Who?' I asked, concerned for my baby.

'Vanessa Brown, her sister and one of the younger boys. I have to do my bit in the community you know. I won't risk my daughter, or my cousin, being left with a paedophile. I'm not a complete monster.' He smirked.

He was a monster, but I knew he wouldn't let harm come to Ella, so I believed he was telling the truth. Besides, he was only happy when he was destroying lives, so I doubted he'd want another predator encroaching on his turf.

I was sure that Jon wouldn't have let Bess stay at the Brown's. A drunk he might be, but he was a good dad. He'd never put Bess at risk. I also felt some relief in the knowledge that Bess was friends with Ella. When Bess was with Ella, Chrissie would be protecting them both. She'd never let a pervert get anywhere near them.

There was a tiny knock on the door.

'What the fuck?' Richard jumped and spun around so fast he almost lost his balance. I could see a boy through the door. 'What are you doing out of the car you fuckin' freak? Get back in there now.'

I heard the boy scuttle across whatever room or hallway was outside mine and slam another door shut. Then the dogs started barking.

'Who was that?' I asked.

'Nobody.'

'Was it Kevin?' I asked him bravely.

'Peter.' He corrected me.

He pushed me down on to the mattress and started to undo his trousers. He stopped, remembering that this wouldn't get a reaction from me. I refused to fight him or react in any way. My lack of emotion wasn't a turn on for him. I knew this and it was my only weapon against him. The man was a vile predator who lived his life abusing women and anyone he considered weak. I wouldn't be weak.

Instead of raping me, he masturbated loudly and left his mess on the floor as a reminder to me of what he could do. Then he left, and I was alone again.

Chapter 3

Peter Lawrence

Richard took me to a house in the woods. It was surrounded by trees and had been difficult for him to get his car there, but he'd managed it. He'd told me to wait in the car.

All the windows of the house were boarded up, except for one small one which was too high to see through. Alsatian dogs were guarding the house; I knew they were police dogs that Richard had borrowed from work.

I wasn't sure why he'd brought me here, but I knew better than to question him. I didn't want to question him anyway; he was all I had.

He went into the derelict house, and I thought about my family.

My mum left first with my sister Shell, then Debbie went too. I missed Debbie most; she was kind to me sometimes. Next, the police came for Johnny, who'd apparently stabbed an entire family to death. Pretty soon there was just dad and me, then he fucked off as well. I have no idea where he went.

I was fourteen years old and living in a house by myself. Richard was the only person looking out for me. If it wasn't for him, I'd be in a home full of perverts; that's what he told me anyway.

He could be mean at times and would often hit me, but he made sure I was fed and clothed. I'm pretty sure he was paying the rent, it could have been my dad, but I doubted it; he didn't give a shit. Either way, the rent was paid and nobody bothered me.

I got bored of waiting, so I decided to get out of the car and have a look at the house. As I entered, the dogs became alert and I shit myself. There was a closed door and I could hear Richard's voice, so I knocked quietly; it was either face him or the dogs.

When he opened the door, I was sure I saw a woman

behind him. She wore a pink gown and had really messy hair; perhaps she'd just woken up.

He'd told me to get back to the car before he battered me. I had no choice; I had to face the dogs. I ran back to the car and shut the door. They were barking, but they couldn't get to me.

When Richard returned to the car, he was in a better mood. He must have fucked the woman in the pink gown with the messy hair. It made me excited just thinking about it.

'Who was she?' I asked him as he started the Capri.

'Who was who? Is your imagination running away with you again young Peter?'

'The woman,' I said, 'she had a pink gown and messy hair.'

He laughed. 'You're bloody nuts you are lad. Remember how you imagine things, things you think you've seen. I think you're doing it again.'

I did imagine stuff; voices, a beautiful woman who appeared in my dreams, conversations that didn't happen. But I was sure I didn't imagine this. There had been a woman there.

I knew it was best to leave it now, or I'd earn myself a beating.

When he dropped me off, he followed me inside.

'What news do you have about the council estate scum?' He asked me with a twinkle in his eye.

My job was to keep tabs on three girls; Ella Parker, Bess Holland who lived next door, and Nessa Brown. I was to report back to him with any information I had about them or their families.

He had once told me that Ella Parker was his daughter. I never believed him; she was Chris Parker's daughter, everybody knew that. Why would Chris Parker be looking after Richard's kid?

He also told me that he'd had Nessa put into care with her brother and sister because their dad was a paedophile. He did it to protect the girls, especially Ella. Things like that showed me he wasn't a bad person. In fact, he was a bit of a hero if you asked me. He looked after me when my own parents abandoned me and taken the Brown's away from their pervert dad. He was alright, just had a bit of a temper on him.

Richard always said I would suffer in a bad way if I was ever to tell a soul what we discussed. I believed him, but I had nobody to tell anyway.

I tried to think of something to report.

'They hang around with the Bailey boys a lot,' I told him.

The Bailey boys were trouble and had seen me off a few times. Nessa was obsessed with Simon Bailey.

'Good work,' he said, and threw a couple of coins at me like I was a fuckin' tramp.

He stood up, and for a minute I thought he was going to embrace me. I felt awkward, but he didn't embrace me. He slapped me hard across the face, and as he did, I bit down on my lip and immediately tasted blood.

'What was that for?' I asked.

'That's for following me when I told you to stay in the car. I'm the only thing keeping you out of a home or off the streets. You'd be dead if it wasn't for me, so you better bloody do as I tell you.'

With that, he walked out of the house.

'Fucking bastard,' I muttered to myself.

I watched him through the window as he walked across the green; he was right, I didn't have anybody else. Nobody would even notice if I disappeared off the face of the earth.

I looked towards next door where Bess Holland lived with her dad. There was a street light in front of our houses that kept me company in the darkness of night. It shone an orange light into my bedroom and probably did the same into hers.

She used to play with me on the green, but since she'd made friends with Ella Parker, she barely spoke to me. Ella was too big for her boots. She controlled Bess and Nessa, and I was sure Bess would have been my friend if it wasn't for her.

I lay on the bed thinking of all the times I'd had a slap across the face or a dig in the ribs. It didn't matter; it never hurt for long.

What did hurt, was a memory from a long time ago of a beautiful lady who always smelled like flowers and dressed up like a film star. She appeared in my dreams often and sometimes came to me when I was awake too. Or at least, she came into my thoughts. Who was she? I felt a sense of loss when she came into my head. I hurt for her, but I had no idea why.

I thought I felt an arm around me as I started to drift off to sleep. I could smell her floral perfume; it made me feel safe and a little less lonely.

Chapter 4

Helen Ellis

The years were flying by and nothing had changed. I was still a verbal and physical punch bag for my husband.

I'd never known any different as an adult. Richard had been in my life since my teenage years and I'd just accepted that this was how life was. I couldn't escape so I just had to get on with it.

At least I had a roof over my head, food in my belly and clothes on my back. And I had my boys. They were worth every bit of pain their father caused me.

Since Jon Holland had been to fix a leak all those years ago, I'd not been allowed visitors to the house. If anything needed fixing Richard would hire someone. He'd be there when they arrived and would stay with them until they'd completed the job. I'd learnt to keep out of the way, never engaging in small talk with any men. I'd avoid eye-contact so that I wouldn't be accused of flirting. I couldn't bear the consequences.

Apart from these occasions, we never had visitors to the house. The only exception was my Aunt Doreen and her visits were rare.

She was coming today though, and I was excited by the prospect of seeing her. It had been so long since I'd had any female company.

My boys were all doing their own thing; Robert and David were both at Manchester University. Robert was studying for a degree in law, and I had no doubt he'd join the police force like his father and his grandparents. David was studying for a business degree; he had no aspirations to follow in his father's footsteps. I was extremely proud of them both.

Young Richard was a handful. He was difficult. He didn't want to go to college, he wanted a job but didn't want to work. He was lazy and got himself in trouble on numerous occasions.

His father had often brought him home, and then I would get it in the neck for not being able to control him. 'You're too caught up in your own world and too selfish to have children,' he'd tell me.

After his father had finished tearing me down, young Richard would accuse me of being weak and pathetic. I now had two of them throwing their weight about.

My two older boys had started to defend me, and Richard didn't start if they were about; like every other bully, he was a coward.

The bell rang, and I knew it would be Doreen. I checked my reflection in the mirror as I passed through the hall.

I stared at myself and felt the tears well up. I looked older than my years and my eyes had dark circles under them. I looked exhausted.

I went to let Aunt Doreen in.

'It's been too long,' she cried, as she ran out of her little car to greet me.

Her hair was beautifully coiffured, she was dressed casually and looked well, although she too had aged.

'How are you darling?' she asked.

'All good,' I lied.

'Come on; let's get in and get a nice cup of tea.'

Sat with cups of tea, we chatted as though no time had passed us by. I was saddened when we worked out it had been at least five years since her last visit.

I knew she would be under orders on what to talk about and I suppose I was too. I couldn't mention what my life was really like.

'So, what's been happening out in the big bad world? Do you see anyone?'

She was hesitant at first.

'There was a shooting on the estate recently, at The Lion pub. A couple of people caught bullets. Jon Holland and some lad called Peter Lawrence.'

'Oh my gosh,' I said. I wondered momentarily if Richard had anything to do with it. He was convinced I'd had an affair with Jon. Maybe it was revenge.

'Jon's ok,' she continued, 'the bullet skimmed his face; it will probably leave a mark, but he's very lucky.'

'Good God! I bet Madge was worried sick?' I said shaking my head. Doreen knew Richard's cousin; it had been her who told me when Bess was born; Richard never spoke to me much about his family. I think he liked to keep me separate from them.

'Madge hasn't been seen for years Helen,' she said. She sounded surprised that I didn't know. 'She left Jon and disappeared off the face of the earth. She packed up two bags, one for her and one for Bess. Said she'd be back to collect Bess the next day but never returned. The poor girl was heartbroken.'

I was shocked. I couldn't believe that Madge would just leave her child. I didn't really know the woman, but even so, I couldn't imagine any mother walking out like that.

There was a noise from the hall, and David walked in.

'Hi Aunt Doreen,' he said cheerfully and greeted his great aunt with a kiss.

Doreen asked him about university, and he told her all about his studies. She asked if he had a girlfriend, he said 'a few' and this made me smile. He was a handsome, intelligent young man; he'd make a good husband for someone one day.

Time flew by and soon it was time for Doreen to leave. I was sad that I had to say goodbye and made her promise not to leave it so long between visits. I doubted she had much choice.

Later that night, I thought about the conversation that we'd had today, and I suddenly wondered if Richard still kept his journal. Maybe he knew something about Madge's disappearance. She had tried to help me by arranging for Christine to be in The Lion that day. Maybe he'd got wind of that.

I had stopped reading his journal years ago. At first, it gave me a good insight into what he was like; I found comfort in knowing that it was him who had something wrong with him, not me. But after a while, his entries scared me; I decided I'd rather not know too much about the monster I was married to.

I lay in bed that night, thinking about what I knew, trying to put the pieces together. I looked at the clock; it was 2 am. I couldn't sleep so I decided to go downstairs and make a cup of tea.

I started to head downstairs but the house was cold, so I went back for my dressing gown. I bumped straight into David.

'You frightened me half to death,' I whispered, not wanting to wake my other boys up.

'Sorry,' he said, 'I couldn't sleep, I'm going out for a walk.'

The thought disturbed me.

'You're going for a walk at two in the morning?' I was puzzled.

'Yeah,' he muttered.

I didn't want to argue with him, so I let it go. I didn't like it though.

After he left, I filled the big copper kettle and placed it on the cooker. I took a box of matches out of a drawer and lit the hob.

I sat down at the big kitchen table and waited patiently for the kettle to boil. I couldn't see a thing out of the windows as it was pitch black outside. There were no streetlights here which was adding to my unsettling thoughts.

Madge Holland was on my mind. I hadn't known her well, but I knew she wouldn't leave a child. I couldn't pass judgement on their marriage, but Jon had seemed like such a good man. I can't imagine she would just disappear without warning.

I suspected that this was Richard's doing and I couldn't sit still.

I had to read his journals. I just hoped they were still here.

I went to Richard's study. He always kept it locked, but

I had a spare key that he didn't know about. Richard told me he needed the office to keep confidential work documents in and it was strictly out of bounds. It had been my dad's office and it reminded me of him. I hated the idea of never being allowed in there again, so I'd kept the spare key a secret. I used to sneak in sometimes when Richard was away so I could feel close to my dad. It had been such an occasion when I stumbled across the journals

I took some deep breaths as I stood in front of the door, key in hand. It had been years since I'd dared go in; Richard's visits were too unpredictable, and I hadn't wanted to risk it. He would kill me if he caught me in there.

I started shaking uncontrollably as I put the key in the lock; I had to steady my arm with my other hand. Once I'd unlocked the door, I ran in and shut the door behind me quickly. I took a minute to calm my nerves.

The study hadn't changed one bit since I was a little girl. It was small with a desk made of rich dark wood in the corner. On the desk was a large, old-fashioned telephone and a lamp. I went over and flicked it on.

The click of the switch was so loud that it made me jump. The room had one full-length window, covered with heavy Victorian drapes that had to be tied open with a big thick rope. I was glad the curtains were closed. I couldn't cope with the idea that someone might be able to see in.

The Adrenalin was pumping through my body as I searched the office for his journals. I couldn't find them anywhere and thought he might have got rid of them or burned them. I was about to give up hope when I remembered dad's safe.

It was hidden behind the small bookshelf which could be easily moved. I hesitated because if he could tell I'd been in there, the consequences would be unthinkable.

I went for it anyway. Dad had set the code as my birthday and luckily, Richard hadn't bothered to change it.

The heavy door opened and there in the safe sat lots of books of all shapes and sizes. His journals.

I stared at the books. Where would I start? I grabbed one,

and as I did, I heard the door open behind me.

The hairs on the back of my neck stood on end, and I felt frozen to the spot. I couldn't even turn around.

'What the hell are you doing?'

His face looked so angry; it was that of a mad man. He was angrier than I'd ever seen him in his life. I braced myself as he launched himself toward me.

Chapter 5

Madge Holland

I'd slammed my aunt's car into reverse, but I was so shaken up that I could hardly drive straight. I reversed onto a grass verge and the car stalled.

I watched him get out of his car and pass the beautiful old-fashioned gas light that was on its original black lead post and glass holder. I rapidly tried to re-start the car.

My god, why was I so scared? He was my cousin, my family.

He pulled open the door of the car and calmly told me to get out.

I glanced toward the letter which I'd left on the passenger seat. I reached out to get it, but it was too late, he'd seen it. He dragged me from the car and reached in to retrieve it. He placed it carefully in his inside pocket without even looking at it.

'What do you want?' He asked, his eyes piercing, his mouth hard and tight.

I was in no position to make anything up; I couldn't think that fast.

'Chrissie Parker gave me a letter for Helen. You have it now, so I'll go. I need to get back for Bess.'

I took a step towards my car, but he stopped me, grabbing both of my shoulders.

'Why would you bring a letter here for Helen from Christine Parker? You've never been here, have you?'

'No.' I said meekly.

'Why were you coming to my house with a letter from her, for Helen? You don't even speak to her.'

I explained that I'd just bumped into her.

'You have the letter.' I pointed towards his jacket pocket.

He was rubbing his chin. 'Walk to my car.' His tone was cold.

'I need to get back Richard.' I was almost pleading.

'Back? To that loser Jon? Did you know he was fucking Helen while you were pregnant?' He was grinning.

I didn't believe anything he said, but he still planted doubt in my head.

He led me roughly by the arm to where his Ford Capri was parked, just outside the gates of their huge house.

I tried to pull away, but he was strong and held on to me hard. He forced me into the passenger side of the car.

'Please Richard, I need to get back to Bess. What are you doing?'

His face looked crazy as he shut the door and walked around to the other side. I thought about opening the passenger door and running like hell, but I knew I didn't stand a chance. Where would I run?

He leant across to open the glove compartment and took out a gun. I felt the piss trickle down my leg.

'Scared?' *He started laughing.*

He told me to get down into the footwell. He started to drive. I couldn't tell where we were going, but he must have entered the grounds of his house judging by the direction.

'Talk to me,' *he demanded.*

'I know that Peter Lawrence is really Kevin Parker.' *I don't know why I said it.*

He slammed the breaks on, and the car swerved slightly.

'Who have you spoken to about that?'

He grabbed my hair hard.

'Nobody. I promise you.' *I tried to convince him.* *'Please, I'm sorry. I will never tell a soul, I swear.'*

I was begging, pleading with all my might, but I knew he was enjoying the power.

I didn't know what else to do. I didn't know how to get out of this or how to play his game. I was trapped.

It wasn't long before he pulled up. I remember thinking we might be going into his house and that Helen would be there and everything would be ok.

He used his tie to blindfold me. Guns? Blindfolds? I thought this kind of thing only happened in films, but I was wrong. I was being kidnapped.

He pulled me roughly out of the car and pushed me forward, I had no idea where I was going.

My nerves took over and I started to feel sick. I took deep breaths as the horrible tasting liquid started to rise to my throat. I tried to swallow it down, but I couldn't, and I threw up.

I got a hard slap across my face for the inconvenience.

He guided me through what I assumed was a house or a barn; I wasn't sure. It felt damp and cold, and I shuddered. I felt vulnerable, I felt exposed, and I felt weak.

We went through some doors, took my blindfold off and stood in front of me with the gun. We were in a small room with a mattress on the floor and a sink in the corner. I didn't know it then, but this room was about to become my prison.

'Why are you doing this?' I asked.

I still believed he would let me go and that he was just trying to scare me, He was doing a good job.

'You're supposed to be my family, but you're working with those two fuckers. The scumbag slut and my neurotic wife. I know you arranged it with Helen to meet at The Lion the night my children were born. You're jealous because your fucking alcoholic husband is obsessed with my beautiful wife. You know why, don't you? Because you're a frumpy old bag. Look at the fucking state of you. No wonder he's constantly pissed, you probably look more attractive after a few pints, you ugly bitch.'

I could hardly believe the vile crap that came out of his mouth, but I was in no position for a showdown. Anything I said would set me up for a fall. I just stayed silent in the hope he would calm down and let me go home.

Instead, he smacked me hard across the face. It was so hard that I fell backwards on to a mattress.

'Get your fucking clothes off you whore; I'll give you what that limp dick, Jon Holland, can't give you.'

As frightened as I was, I was not going to give Richard any more power than he already had over me. As he ripped my panties off me, I helped him. I even smiled at him as he put his hands on my breast. I closed my eyes and allowed him to do what he wanted. I knew I didn't have a choice, so why resist. I knew he wanted power over me, that's what rape was about. I wasn't going to give it to him. I wasn't going to struggle or cry or scream out. If I didn't give him the power he wanted over me, he'd get bored and let me go. I'd be useless to him. As vile as it was, and as sickening as it felt, I also had a sense of power. Richard thrived on controlling and weakening people. If I stayed strong, then I'd surely win. What I didn't know was just how strong I'd have to be.

The act worked. He lost interest and walked away dissatisfied with my reaction. He never raped me again. I told myself it hadn't been rape, that I'd let him do it. In a way it made me feel better, like I had some control.

Over the years, he tried different things to wear me down; masturbating on the floor, beating me, telling me lies about Jon and Bess. But I stuck to my plan and stayed strong. And all the while, I prayed for the day when Richard Ellis would get his comeuppance.

****

I sat up and looked around. There was nothing much to look at except a few bits that he'd left for me over the years. I had a couple of books, including a Jackie Collins novel that I'd read over and over again. The room had barely changed since that day he had brought me here.

More years had passed, I'd lost count of the days, and I was near giving up. Any hope I was holding on to was fading. I saw no light. I saw no escape.

The night was silent except for the wildlife that was never far away from me. I wondered what time it was. Not that it mattered. There was a full moon tonight and it shone through the window, lighting up the room. Even though my existence was so miserable, I appreciated the moonlight. It made me feel something inside. It wasn't hope, it wasn't fear, and it wasn't happiness; it was just a reminder that I was alive.

A sudden noise made the hair on the back of my neck stand up. There was someone in the house.

He had never been here in the middle of the night before. Maybe he'd forgotten something. Maybe he wanted to finally kill me.

Maybe it wasn't him. Maybe it was the police. Maybe someone had finally found me. So many thoughts ran through my head. I was scared and excited all at once.

The door flew open and, in the moonlight, I could see a shadow, the shadow of a man a very young man.

We stared at each other for what felt like a long time.

'Who are you?' he asked.

His tone was gentle.

'I'm Madge. Madge Holland,' I whispered.

Again, there was silence.

'I heard them talking about you today.'

'Who?' I was still frozen to the spot. 'Who was talking about me?'

'It's ok, don't worry,' he said; 'I'm not here to hurt you.'

He held out both his hands towards me; it was a friendly gesture, he was letting me know he meant no harm.

'How long have you been here, do you even know?'

I shook my head.

He was young, he was dark, and he was handsome. I took his hands and a heat went down my face, into my breasts, into my stomach and ended up somewhere between my legs.

I was tired of being alone, tired of never seeing daylight and tired of having no one to hold me.

The moonlight shone on his beautiful, tanned face. I'm not sure what had come over me, but I wanted this boy. I needed this boy and I needed him now.

Like the caged animal I was, I pounced. I kissed him hard on the lips. He responded, and I pulled him into me.

'It's been so long,' I sighed, the desire almost bringing me to tears.

'I've never done this before,' he muttered, as he kissed my neck slowly.

'Don't worry,' I whispered. 'I'll show you.'

He wore a velour tracksuit with a zipped top and matching bottoms.

I unzipped his top and put both my hands underneath it. I could feel his bare skin on my hands. I stroked his smooth chest, slowly taking in the feel of another human being and I brushed his nipples with the edge of my thumbs.

I removed his top and threw it to the floor.

'I just want to feel you. I'm not sure if you're real or if I've finally gone crazy.'

'I'm real,' he murmured, kissing my neck. His mouth was warm and wet as he sucked my skin sending my whole body into a frenzy.

I threw my head back as he lifted up my night dress.

I stood naked in front of him, knowing he'd never done it before. It gave me feelings I'd long forgotten.

I stepped back to the mattress on the floor and lay back like some whore who needed a good seeing to. I was out of my mind, but I didn't care.

'Will you kiss me here?' I asked pointing between my legs. He didn't hesitate. His kisses were soft and sensual, his tongue wet and warm.

I lay back and thought of all the years I had spent here reading the dirty parts in the Jackie Collin's book. Now here I was acting as though I was one of her characters.

He was enjoying himself and was exploring now with his fingers, moaning as he did so. I guided his hand to where it needed to be, and he stroked and licked until I gave in to the torment. I arched my body hard against his face as I reached orgasm, moaning loudly.

He moved on top of me, and I felt the warmth of his manhood as it found its way inside me. We moved together frantically, pushing hard into each other. The fact it was the first time that he'd been inside a woman turned me on even more.

He moaned, and I felt him explode inside me.

Chapter 6

Peter Lawrence

Richard's requests were getting more and more questionable. I was beginning to feel uncomfortable about what he wanted me to do.

He'd had the Bailey family evicted and moved down south somewhere, so they were out of the way. Now he wanted me to stalk the Parkers and make them scared. This wasn't easy as Ella had two feisty brothers who wouldn't think twice about knocking the shit out of me. They weren't a bad family, and it felt wrong to be messing with them.

The youngest child, Josie, was doted on by them all. It was as though they had got a big ball of cotton wool and wrapped her in it. It didn't do her any favours as you needed your wits about you on this estate.

Josie was approaching puberty and was a pretty young girl. She was fair whereas Ella was dark. She was quiet whereas Ella was feisty. She was sweet whereas Ella was a twat.

Richard was interested in Josie in a very unhealthy way. He had once told me what he wanted to do to her. It left me a bit disturbed; she was still a kid.

He wanted me to watch Josie; said he was going to do what he'd done to her mother. I asked what he meant, and he wouldn't explain. He wanted me to tell him when she was alone.

I think he'd slept with Chris Parker against her will and that Ella was the result. But if I questioned him, he'd say I was making it up, and that he'd never told me that Ella was his daughter in the first place. It was so confusing, and it was difficult to know what was true and what was a lie. I was tired of trying to please him. If he wasn't happy, which was most of the time, then he would hurt me.

I decided to go to The Lion to see if the girls were in there. I wanted the girls to like me. I wanted to show them that I meant no harm, but whenever I tried to talk to them, I'd just call them slags or scum. I didn't mean it; it was just to get a reaction and to make sure they knew I existed.

I walked up the main road that was surrounded by trees. For a council estate, it was kind of beautiful.

Jon Holland was outside the pub with the rest of his cronies; Bess was with them. I was dying to say hello, but instead, I coughed the phlegm up from my lungs and spat on the floor like the disgusting animal they thought I was. I put my head down and walked by as though they were the disgusting ones.

I entered The Lion, and the atmosphere was tense. There had recently been some trouble with gangs from another estate, and rumour was that they were after the landlady's son Conny.

'What do you fuckin' want?' was the greeting I got when I approached the bar.

Lizzie Concannon, the mouthy Landlady, who liked the sound of her own voice more than the sound of the fucking tills ringing, would never welcome me. She always had a snide remark to put me down. The fucking piece of shit.

'Can I have a pint?'

'You can if you fucking ask properly.'

I felt stupid. Why did they all do this to me? I only wanted to be part of it all.

Bess and Nessa had moved into the pub and were sat in the corner, looking at me like I was shit on their shoe. I had a good mind to make something up about the slags so Richard would kill them both.

Jon Holland was approaching the bar when suddenly, there was the loudest bang I'd ever heard in my life.

A Ford Escort had been driven into the front of the pub and whoever had been driving it had fired off some shots through the window.

Jon Holland screamed as a bullet hit him in the eye, or so I thought at the time. Bess's scream was chilling. I ran over to see if I could help, but then I got fucking shot right in my fucking leg.

The day couldn't get any worse. I should have stayed in fucking bed.

Chapter 7

Helen Ellis

It was my son, Richard, running at me, not my husband as I'd first expected.

'What the fuck are you doing? This is dad's private study,' he said, as he knocked me to the floor.

'This was also my father's private study,' I defended myself. 'My father built it,' I reminded him, with defiance.

'Dad said your father was nothing but a fuckin' nigger.'

My blood was starting to boil.

I got off the floor. He was circling me.

How, after all I had been through and all that I believed in, had I gone so wrong to bring up one of my children like this. My mother would turn in her grave if she could hear him now.

'I'll ask you again. What the fuck are you doing in here?' His tone was menacing, and I had the same feelings that I had when my husband was aggressive.

I couldn't answer him. I certainly couldn't say I was looking through his father's journals. I had no doubt that he would tell him. Then there would be trouble.

'I thought I heard a noise,' I lied.

'Liar! You're looking for something.'

He moved towards me, and I prepared myself for the attack. My defence mechanism was weak, but it wasn't dead.

'One more time mother. What are you doing in here?'

'What the fuck has it got to do with you?' came a voice. I turned towards the source.

David stood at the door. He was just in the nick of time; god knows what young Richard would have done to me.

But now I had another problem. They were big, strapping lads and I didn't want to see any trouble between them. I'd rather be the one to take the trouble so that they didn't hurt each other.

'Go to your room mum. Try and get some sleep.' said David.

Part of me wanted to stay and stop them from fighting, part of me was screaming to get out while I had the chance, grateful that I had been saved. I was so exhausted that self-preservation won, and I left the room as quickly as I could.

I knew David wanted to protect me; Richard just wanted to protect himself. They'd probably fight, but they were brothers and they loved each other, so they'd never do any real damage.

I climbed into bed and fell into a deep sleep within seconds.

I didn't expect to wake up to the chaos that greeted me the next morning.

As I went downstairs, my first thought was to have a cup of tea. I froze when I found my husband sitting at the kitchen table, slowly sipping a cup of tea and reading a newspaper as though he did that every morning.

'What's wrong?' My voice shook with trepidation. I knew I wouldn't like the answer.

'What happened here last night?' he asked, and as he did, he stood up and started to pace up and down the kitchen.

'What do you mean?' I decided to play dumb.

'Where are your two youngest sons?'

His edge was so sharp I could feel it slicing the air as he spoke.

'I don't know where they are?' I replied, and I didn't.

'David is in intensive care,' he said. 'That's where one of them is. Care to guess who put him there?'

I gasped and grabbed my neck; I couldn't breathe.

'What's wrong with him, what has Richard done to him? Richard? Please tell me what happened? What's wrong with David?' The knot in my stomach was getting tighter.

'He tried to commit suicide,' said Richard calmly. 'He tried to hang himself in my study of all places'.

This was getting crazy. I knew he had not tried to hang himself.

'Where's Richard?' I asked him again.

He shrugged.

'Who called you?'

He stood up slowly.

'Are you questioning me? Are you calling me a fucking liar Helen?'

I didn't want to deal with his game-playing right now. My energy was low in the very presence of this man. But I had to stay strong. My son needed me, and I needed to get to him, no matter what.

'Where is our son?' I said with more confidence than I felt.

'Are you fucking stupid?' he spat. 'He's in Intensive care, I just told you.'

'Which hospital?'

He started walking towards me, but thankfully, Robert walked through the kitchen door. Normally I would shut up at that point, but I took advantage of his presence.

'Robert, take me to the hospital please?'

'What's happened? he asked blurry-eyed.

'David is in intensive care; your father was about to tell me which hospital,' I said. I hardly dared look at Richard; I'd pay for this later, but for now, I didn't care.

'What's going on dad?' Robert asked with such force; I would have felt proud if I hadn't been so afraid.

'David has had an accident,' Richard said as though he was talking about a neighbour.

'You just said that he tried to commit suicide?' I challenged.

Robert's stance was firm.

'What's happened Dad, can you let us know please?'

'Your brother is at the general hospital on the estate. He was found by Richard in the early hours of this morning, hanging by the rope from my curtains. Thank god young Richard found him and had the decency to call an ambulance. David was unconscious and just minutes away from death. What they were doing in my study at that time of the morning, I'll never know. But it doesn't matter, what matters Is that David is alright.'

He was lying. It was obvious that young Richard had hurt my boy, but I couldn't say anything. If I did, I would have to admit to being in the study and he'd use that against me. I would somehow get the blame.

Right now, I was lucky because Robert was next to me, but that wouldn't always be the case.

'Take me to the hospital please Robert.'

Robert didn't hesitate. 'Go and get yourself ready mum. I'll wait here and then I'll take you to see David'.

I was dressed in a flash and ran back downstairs to find that Robert had gone.

'Is he waiting outside?' I asked my husband as he sat there reading the paper without a care in the world.

'No,' he answered, not even lifting his head.

'I told him I would take you later and that he should make sure his brother is ok before we get there.'

My heart sunk; out of all the years of terrible moments, this had to be the worst.

'Sit down and have a cup of tea; once you've calmed down, I'll take you to him.'

I didn't want to sit down. He'd just told me that my seventeen-year-old son was in intensive care and I wanted to know what had happened. He was badly injured but to what extent? I wanted to see my boy; I wanted to hold his hand. Instead, I was being toyed with by this piece of shit.

'What have the doctors said? Have you been to see him?' My tone was frantic and he was revelling in my anxiety.

Stay calm and don't feed him, I kept telling myself. This could explode, and if it did, I wouldn't be going anywhere. I had to play this right. Always playing and forever losing.

I was sure a normal husband would take their wife's hand and say, 'come on let's go to the hospital.' But he wasn't a normal husband; this wasn't a normal relationship; he wasn't normal.

'Sit down,' he repeated, 'we'll go after you've had a cup of tea.'

'Would it be ok if we go now please? I just want to see if our son is ok.'

His silent response should have told me not to ask again. I wished he would drop dead at the kitchen table. I didn't care what he did anymore.

'Richard can we just go to the hospital please?' My tone was much calmer than I felt inside.

He stood up.

'Do you know why David is in intensive care?' he asked. He was rubbing his hands together.

I knew I was in danger, but I was now past caring.

I humoured him. 'Because he tried to hang himself?'

'Don't be fucking smart Helen. It's your fucking fault that he's in the hospital.'

He stared at me, and I felt pure hatred toward him.

'Not only do you want to make my life hell, but you also want us fighting because of you. You did it with Robert and me ten minutes ago; you're a very dangerous woman. Everyone would get along with one another if it weren't for you.'

I wanted to punch him.

'So, because you were up to no fucking good in my study, the boys have had a huge fight, and young Richard has almost strangled David to death. All because of you.'

I tried to step away from him but found myself getting closer to the cooker. I was feeling stifled.

I pushed him away from me with all my might and he flew backwards onto the floor. He jumped up, brushing himself down, checking for marks on his shirt. I ran to the door, but I wasn't quick enough.

He grabbed my long black hair and pulled me down onto the kitchen floor. As I fell, he got one sly punch into the back of my head. The familiar taste of bile was at the back of my throat. The bile that I'm sure was eating me alive, killing me slowly, just as he was.

This had to stop or one of us was going to get killed. If I had just waited for him to finish his cup of tea and made one myself, this probably wouldn't have happened. I should have known not to ask him again. I really did push my luck with him at times.

I lay on the floor waiting for his next move, which was a hard kick to my legs. I curled up in agony and pulled at his leg to stop him kicking me further. He lay on top of me with his face pushing hard on my face.

'You ever fucking attack me like that again and I will fucking kill you. Do you understand me?'

I had to stop the violence; he was right; it was all around me and I was creating it. It would be better if I wasn't here at all.

Chapter 8

Madge Holland

I woke up in the morning and thought that I had dreamt about David. I lay there for a while thinking about what had happened during the night, but more excited for what was about to happen. David was going to get me out of here. I knew it. I just had to be patient.

'Who are you?' I had asked him as he rolled off me. I wasn't even embarrassed that I'd not asked him before.

'I'm David Ellis,' he said. 'I think it's my dad who locked you up here.' He looked ashamed.

I was mortified. I was his second cousin, and I had given up my body like a sex slave.

'David, I'm so sorry for what just happened. Your dad is my cousin. I feel dreadful. I don't know what came over me. I shouldn't have done that to you. I've been locked up here for so long, I just – '

I burst into tears and started sobbing uncontrollably.

He got up off the mattress quickly. 'Don't cry,' he said softly, 'I don't know how, but I will sort this out. I'm nothing like my father, I promise.'

'Please help me,' I sobbed. 'I want to see my daughter and my husband. I want my life back. Every day I live in hope and now you're my hope.'

'I have to go back to the house. I'll come back for you,' he said.

'No!' I panicked, 'you can't just leave me here, please.'

'Be patient. I promise you there is light at the end of this tunnel. I will get you back to your daughter and husband.'

'When?' I asked desperately.

'As soon as I can. Please, just be patient.'

'Your dad is powerful in the police force,' I reminded him. 'Be careful.'

'I'm not afraid of him.'

His teeth were gritted. I could feel his determination.

'I know, but just be careful.'

He kissed me on the forehead like he was family and then he left.

I fell into a deep sleep feeling better than I had in years.

Now as I waited patiently for David to come back, I was scared I had made the wrong decision in trusting him. What if he never came back? What if it was all a trick, set up by Richard? Maybe he wanted me as a sex slave for his sons.

In the daylight, I realised how stupid my actions had been. For the first time since I'd gotten here, I had a real chance of escaping, and instead of taking the chance to get out, I'd used a seventeen-year-old boy as a sex toy. I must be fucked in the head.

Maybe I deserved to be here after all. I looked around. The walls were peeling more than ever, and the cold, damp brick was becoming more and more visible. There were bits of dried paint that had fallen from the ceiling and landed on the floor. I decided to pick them up, to tidy up a bit. I laughed out loud at my own madness.

Day turned to night and my mind was in overdrive. I began to think that Richard had actually sent David to mess with my head. It was the sort of thing he would do.

'No!' I told myself. He had been so genuine; he can't have been faking it. I'd taken his virginity, and it had been such a beautiful moment. Surely Richard wouldn't want that to happen? He'd want destruction and fear, not the gentle, loving intimacy we'd shared.

But how did he know I was here?

Why hadn't he come back?

Had he told anyone?

I tried to be rational. It had only been a day, and he had told me to be patient.

I took some deep breaths and listened to the sounds my body made. I had found that if I concentrated hard enough on my breathing, it would stop my head going into complete overdrive. I had to stay sane.

Chapter 9

Peter Lawrence

The shooting at The Lion left me with a permanent limp. On top of that, Richard was making demands of me more often than usual and his requests were getting bizarre.

A lifetime of growing up around this man had made me confused. My perspective was skewed; I didn't know what was true, and at times, I didn't even know what was real. I'd be sure something had happened, and it wouldn't have. I had moments of delirium that often took over.

'Remember' he said, 'you're employed by me and one day you will be paid a shed load of money and you'll be out of here for good. You're one very lucky man.'

I asked why he was so interested in the Parkers.

'They owe me for causing me so much stress all my life. They've made me ill, all of them, by keeping my only daughter away from me. Years of torment, I've suffered. I'm being fucking serious Peter. They've all made my life a misery. They've treated you like shit too. They've never treated you with any respect. Who do they fuckin' think they are Peter? They are fucking scum, council estate scum, and one day you'll be away from it all. Free of the fucking stares, free of the taunts, and free of the fuckin slags who think that they're better than you. They took it all away from us son, so it's our turn to destroy them.'

Not long after the shooting at The Lion, the landlady's son, Conny, was killed. Ella had been in a relationship with him and was devastated. I knew that Richard had orchestrated the whole thing. I never worked out how he could put together such elaborate plans and get away with it.

About a year later, Richard carried out what was probably his most vile act by far; the rape of young Josie Parker.

Reluctantly, I was part of the whole set up. I didn't have

a choice and I hadn't known the extent of what Richard had planned.

Ella had landed a job as a chambermaid on the cruise ships and was leaving to travel the world. It was a pretty big deal for someone from our estate. Not many people got the chance to leave.

Lizzie at The Lion had arranged a huge leaving party, and half of the estate was expected to attend.

Richard had me on full alert once he'd got wind of it. I had to report back about who would be there. That was really difficult to do when no fucker would speak to me.

He asked me to watch Josie Parker closely. He wanted to know every move she made.

I'd recently had a beating off the Parker brothers for spying on Josie. I'd been hanging around their house, but I was just doing as I was told. I didn't realise at the time that Richard was setting me up to take the fall for the crime he was about to commit. He was clever and made sure that I'd look like a freak following Josie Parker everywhere like a fucking weirdo.

Josie was a young girl of about fifteen, a child who was losing all her puppy fat and becoming a young woman. Her fair hair was turning darker and her light blue eyes, paler. She was a pretty little thing.

During Ella's party, my job was to entice Josie outside by tricking her into thinking her mother was out there waiting for her. I did as I was asked, not realising what that animal was going to do. I only found out the extent of Josie's ordeal afterwards.

She was found left for dead, raped and battered, in a bush not far from The Lion.

When I heard what had happened, I got out of there. It was my fault; I'd led her right to him. I'd never be able to sleep properly again.

I realised that night that Richard was pure evil. I have no idea why he looked after me. What was the connection? Sure, he'd been fucking my mum, but even after she'd gone, he'd stuck around. Maybe he just worked out I'd be of use to him someday.

I thought about my family, my so-called mother who I had watched Richard fuck over the settee. I'll never forget her pleasurable moans and how much the dirty slag had enjoyed it. My so-called father never even noticed I was there. I didn't even miss them.

I looked up and there was a bright light in the corner of my bedroom; it was the lady with the flowery perfume. She was holding her hands out. I wanted to run into her arms. I was reminded of something; I just didn't know what. I felt safe and loved. I walked towards her, but when I got across the room, she'd gone and once again, I felt alone.

The sickness took over my body and I threw up everywhere, making no effort to run to the bathroom. What was the point?

The knock on the front door made me jump out of my skin. It could only be him; it could only be Richard.

I was shocked to open the door and find one of the Parker boys and the two Bailey brothers standing on my doorstep. Where the fuck had they come from? I thought Richard had got rid of the Baileys?

They seemed friendly, but they made lots of noise about what had happened to Josie. They didn't have to tell me. I already knew; I'd seen the horror of what he'd done to her. I'd never forget it for as long as I lived.

Richard had wanted everyone to think it was me, so of course, everyone did think it was me. I couldn't move out of the house for fear of repercussion. The police were slow in their questioning. Richard had stalled it.

Then, I received a message of forgiveness and an offer of friendship from the three girls. It was all I had ever wanted.

Ella, Nessa and Beth invited me to a seedy hotel near a small village in Manchester.

The council estate scum, as Richard would call them, led me to believe that we could be friends. Why else would they want to meet me? It never occurred to me that I was the number one suspect for the rape of Josie Parker. It never occurred to me they were luring me in.

You hurt one. You hurt them all.

The hotel was dark, and the front was covered in ivy from head to toe. As I opened the huge door, I was beginning to feel apprehensive.

I couldn't believe what I was seeing when I spotted them in the bar. They were sipping shorts, possibly brandy, and they looked like prostitutes. Three fucking prostitutes, whores who were gagging for it. Dressed in leather skirts and tops that revealed half of their tits. I couldn't contain my excitement and was sure everyone in the bar must have seen my dick rise in my pants.

They invited me up to their room. It was covered in damp with deep pink walls and pink flowery curtains. It smelt musty, but I remember thinking it was actually very nice compared to my house.

Nessa Brown pushed me on the bed; she wanted my dick. They all wanted it; I couldn't believe my luck.

The three of them were all over me. Nessa was about to suck me off, but I was going to have to wait because the door of the room burst open.

Richard stood there, looking a fucking mess. I'd never seen him so dishevelled.

I looked at Bess and saw she had a syringe. Then it clicked. They didn't want to fuck me; they wanted to kill me.

I screamed out that Richard had raped Josie. I needed them to know I wasn't to blame. Out of the corner of my eye, I spotted the Bailey brothers. Si Bailey ran in and jumped onto Richard pushing him to the floor.

For a second, I felt an urge to defend the man who had been like a father to me; then I remembered the beatings.

I spotted the empty syringe drop from Bess's hand, and I saw her look at me as though she was willing me not to get it. I was too quick. I made a dive for it and stuck it right in his fucking neck. He died instantaneously.

Chapter 10

Helen Ellis

Richard made me wait three days before he let me go to the hospital to be with David.

I could no longer see the good in my husband. I knew I hated him. I'd tried for years to focus on his good side, but the bad had outweighed the good for a long time now.

At the hospital, we were greeted by the doctor who was looking after David, Dr Pickering. He gave me a smile and asked me to take a seat. I was conscious of Richard's glare. No doubt he'd accuse me of flirting with the doctor. I wanted to cry.

Dr Pickering explained that David had ligature strangulation which was a very unusual way of trying to commit suicide. He had lost consciousness, but his neck wasn't broken. I started crying as he said it. I was so relieved. He went on to say that there was haemorrhaging near where the cord had been and that he was lucky to be alive. He had a very sore throat, but would be moved out of intensive care later that day now he was more stable.

I wasn't prepared for what I saw. My beautiful boy was in agony, his eyes puffy and red, his face bruised and swollen.

Young Richard had meant business. This wasn't just a fight between two brothers; this was one brother wanting the other dead. I was appalled at my youngest son and apologised to my mother in my head.

How different my life would have been if my parents were still here.

I looked at my husband. It dawned on me that he could have had something to do with their death. I wouldn't put anything past him.

I leant over kissed David with tears streaming down my face.

'I'm so sorry,' I managed to say through my tears.

'Jesus! Don't be so fuckin' dramatic.' Richard's wicked tongue couldn't help itself. 'No wonder this has happened. If you hadn't made him such a girl, he would have fought back.'

'He is a real man, Richard. He has self-control,' I spat. 'It's a good job he didn't fight back, or we could have had two of our sons in a hospital bed.'

'If it wasn't for you wanting them to fight over you, this would never have happened,' Richard sneered.

'Get out!' David mumbled from his bed.

There comes a time when your child's word is stronger than the bully stood opposite you.

'You heard him. Get out!' I said gritting my teeth. I knew I'd suffer later, but right now, I was past caring.

'I beg your pardon?' He laughed. If I didn't know him better, I would have thought it was a nervous laugh.

'Get out!' I repeated with conviction.

He hesitated momentarily and then left David and me alone on the ward. It was full of people taking their last breaths, full of bereft families who weren't as lucky as I was.

I couldn't believe David was here. Richard had been right; it was because of me. And I was going to put an end to this mess one way or another.

'What happened?' I asked my son.

'He pulled the cord off the curtains and tried to strangle me with it.,' he explained. 'I couldn't get him off. It was like he was in a trance. It was terrifying. He must have snapped out of it when I passed out because he brought me here and left. I woke up in here with wires everywhere, not knowing where I was.'

'Don't worry,' I tried to reassure him, 'you're in the best place now, and Dr Pickering said you are going to be ok.'

'Mum?' he said seriously. 'Do you remember the day we got lost in the woods and heard those dogs barking?'

I nodded, not sure if he was having a reaction to the drugs they had pumped into him.

'Well, I heard you and Aunt Doreen talking about a

missing woman, Madge?'

I didn't know where this was going so I just nodded.

'Well, it just made me think of that day. The fuss dad made because Richard said he saw a house. The beating he gave you for going there. And I just knew. I just knew she must be in there.'

I was totally gobsmacked, but I listened to what he had to say.

'That's why I went for a walk that night. I had to know. And I was right mum; he's been holding her captive all these years. She's living in squalor, and she's a mess. I promised I'd go back for her and I didn't. We have to help her.'

'Jesus Christ! I can't believe what I'm hearing.'

I knew Richard was behind Madge's disappearance, I just knew it. I stood up and started pacing up and down the ward.

I couldn't get my head around it. That man had kept a woman locked up like a prisoner in my back garden, while he kept me prisoner up in the house.

I had to set us both free.

'Please don't do anything yet; it's not safe. I'll be out soon,' David whispered.

'I should just call the police. Surely your father doesn't have that amount of influence that he can do anything he bloody wants?'

'Please don't do that, he has nearly every person in there working for him one way or another, he will find out mum; please don't do that?'

'I'll talk to Robert,' I said, 'he'll help me get her out.'

I didn't wait for my husband to come back for me. I was done, it was over. When you see your child in a hospital bed like that, you get a sense of perspective. Was I afraid? Yes, but then I always was afraid, so it made no difference. I felt a strong sense that one day I would be free from all this.

I saw that Richard had left his coat on the back of the hospital chair next to David's bed. He had left his wallet in it which had a handful of notes inside. I put the money in my handbag and decided to find a hotel for the night to clear my head.

The whole idea of defying Richard made me feel anxious and sick to the pit of my stomach. I knew the outcome wouldn't be good; then again, no outcome with Richard was ever good.

I told my son I would see him later and left the hospital by the back entrance where I flagged down a taxi.

The taxi driver was an old grey-haired man with a big grey moustache.

'Where to love?' His eyes smiled as he spoke.

It was getting late and I didn't know the area, so I asked him to recommend a reasonable hotel and he started driving.

We drove through the huge council estate that had somehow become a tangled web, woven by my husband.

In the distance, I could hear sirens. Immediately, I thought Richard had sent the police out to find me. I tasted the hot bile at the back of my throat.

The old man muttered in the front seat. His eyes were kind as they looked at me in the mirror. 'You alright love?'

'I will be,' I said, 'I will be.'

And a warm feeling of calm came over me. The feeling of peace. I knew I would soon be escaping the clutches of Richard Ellis.

Chapter 11

Madge Holland

I hadn't sat up or eaten for days. Waiting for David and him not coming back for me had taken its toll and I'd given up all hope.

Days went by, followed by the nights. I only got out of bed to use the disgusting toilet that was a bucket at the back of the room. Richard hadn't been lately, and it was starting to stink.

I slept and I slept, yet I felt so weak. I didn't see any reason to stay strong anymore. The more I thought about David, the more I thought it was all part of Richard's destructive plan.

It seemed like weeks ago since he stole into the room in the middle of the night and made me feel human for a minute. It had soon passed and now I wished I would just die. It had made me feel worse than I'd ever felt in all these years. I couldn't help but feel rejection and disappointment.

Just as I began to cry again, I heard a noise outside. I listened hard and could hear someone shouting my name. Was it my mind playing tricks? Was it the wind?

Then I heard it again. 'Madge? Madge?'

I could definitely hear a woman's voice calling for me.

I didn't move off the bed. I hoped and prayed that I would finally be free, free from here and free from him.

The door to the room flew open and she stood there. She looked afraid and almost bewildered. Her face had aged and she looked worn out, like someone who had lived through hell. But she was still so beautiful.

I threw myself at the dark angel standing in front of me, and she pulled me close to her, holding me so tightly, making me feel so safe. It was a moment I'd never forget in my life. The dark angel had come to rescue me. I could feel the genuine love and warmth, and there was no mistaking it; she was real.

'David sent me,' she explained. 'He couldn't come himself.' And she went on to explain what had happened to her son.

'Let's get you into the house before we do anything else,' she said.

'Where is he?' I asked.

'I don't know where he is and I no longer care. I've changed the locks at the house, so he can't get in. My other son Robert is on his way from Leeds Police Headquarters to help. Can you walk to the house?'

She had a beautiful aura about her.

'I'll do whatever it takes,' I said

Helen held my hand tightly and looked straight into my eyes.

'It isn't far, but it's through the woods, so you'll need to take care and stay strong.'

The cold night air took my breath away. I hadn't been outside for over a decade, and it made me dizzy, but she held me up.

'Come on Madge. Say 'I've got this', say it out loud,' she said.

'I've got this,' I repeated.

She smiled; 'Yes you have. Come on.'

Every step we took was painful, but she whispered in my ear the whole way; 'You've got this.'

After what seemed like hours, I could see the house lit up in the dark. I was ecstatic.

Helen quickly got her keys out and led me through a huge front door. The house was warm and welcoming, and there was a beautiful feeling about it. It made me feel calm just like she did.

'Come and sit down here. I'll make you a hot tea and bring you a blanket. Robert will only be a few hours; he'll know what to do.'

I smiled, but I couldn't speak.

She brought me a blanket and lit the big fire. She tucked my feet up on her luxurious sofa. The soft touch from her warm, gentle hands gave me hope, as she stroked my head lovingly.

A loud bell rang in the hall and I saw fear in Helen's eyes.

'I'm not expecting anybody,' her voice trembled.

I started to feel anxious and my breathing was becoming shallow. 'Could it be Robert?' I asked her.

'No,' she replied, 'he won't be here for hours yet.'

Helen went to the front door to see who was ringing her bell at what must have been the huge gates. I had a flashback of the huge gates with the old gas light that stood alone as if guarding the big house.

She ran back into the house and grabbed her keys, pulling a big lever which I assumed would open the gates.

I heard another female voice, screaming at the front door. 'Where is he?' Where is that vile fuckin' bastard?'

Seconds later, I was face to face with a distraught Christine Parker.

When she saw me, she froze on the spot.

It was only an hour ago that I'd given up hope of ever seeing anyone again. Now I was in a beautiful, luxurious house with two women. Two women who were a massive part of the tangled web that I had been caught in for so long.

'He raped my daughter.'

She wasn't telling anyone in particular; she was just stating the fact.

The three of us were silent. There was confusion, anger, fear. Nobody quite knew what to say.

Then Richard Ellis appeared in the doorway, holding a gun. He stopped dead in his tracks when he saw Christine Parker and me in his living room.

'How's Josie?' he asked Chrissie, his evil grin playing with her soul.

'You know how she is; she has wounds that will never go away. You fucking animal.'

He pointed the gun towards her.

Helen shouted. 'No, Richard, please.'

He turned his attention to Helen. He circled her and got close up to her face. She went pale and was visibly shaken.

'Where the fuck have you been? And why can't I get in my own house.'

'Maybe it's because you're a fucking animal,' Christine Parker yelled at him.

'You're the fucking animal,' he hissed. 'You're the cunt who danced like a whore to get my cock, then stole my fucking daughter from me.'

He pointed the gun right at her.

'Dance you fucking bitch, show my wife and cousin how you danced for me.'

This silenced her.

'Dance I said.' He was enjoying the fear on all of our faces. I wanted to tell her to dance.

He grabbed Christine Parker by her hair and threw her hard on the floor. He kicked her in her back and waved the gun, taking turns to point it in each of our faces.

Christine screamed at him. 'The girls are going to fucking kill Peter tonight and all along it was you.'

'Baby Kevin you mean?' he said grinning. 'I don't care if they kill that freak. He's been the bane of my fucking life that backward twat. I should have let him burn in the fire with his slag of a mother.'

Christine scrambled back to her feet and was clearly in agony. It was as if she suddenly realised the danger we were all in. She was very silent, very calm.

'I will shoot your fucking brains out, you fucking whore, do you hear me?' He started his attack on Christine again. 'You should have looked after your kids better. I told you and that fucking prick of a husband what I was going to do to her. You didn't even protect her; you allowed it to happen. She didn't dance for me like you did though. She was frightened to fucking death.' He laughed. 'She was a wriggler though, like you. She did a lot of wriggling.'

That was it there and then; she didn't care about the consequences. He'd enraged her. You could hurt a mother all her life, but never hurt her child. She lunged straight at him.

I covered my face with my hands. I couldn't bear it.

I heard the shots; there were three of them.

Richard ran out of the house leaving us to deal with the aftermath.

I didn't know it at the time, but within hours, he'd be dead.

Chapter 12

Helen Ellis

He was going to shoot her. He'd raped her, he'd raped her daughter, and now he was going to end her life.

I had to stop him. I knew what I had to do. I wasn't scared anymore.

I threw myself between them and screamed as he pulled the trigger.

He shot me and I fell to the floor.

Christine Parker was holding my hand and I felt the same electricity that I'd felt all those years ago. It ran through my hand, up my arm and into my soul.

'Please Helen. Please don't go, don't you leave us. Don't let him do this.'

Madge covered me with the blanket I'd used to cover her. I felt a pain in my stomach, but it was no different to the other blows he'd dealt me. The only difference this time was the amount of blood, it was everywhere.

I saw my mum and dad standing over me and I wasn't sure how they'd got into my lounge. It looked as though they were talking, but I couldn't make out their words. I felt the heat, the warmth of them trying to protect my soul. Was I hallucinating or were they really here with me in my final moments?

My vision was blurry; there were moments of light and there were moments of darkness. I thought of my boys and pictured each one of their faces in my head.

Hot tears rolled into my mouth. The taste was comforting; it had always reminded me that to feel pain, you had to be alive. I'd felt enough pain.

I had a beautiful feeling as though someone had cut away big chains that had been shackled to my ankles, my wrists and my neck for most of my life. I felt as though I was floating, moving closer and closer toward sleep.

In the background, I could hear two women crying,

willing me to hold on. I opened my eyes and looked straight into Christine Parker's eyes.

'It's ok,' I said. 'I want to go; I want to be free.'

And then I was…

Part 3

Chapter 1

Ella Parker 1990s

I was really falling for Giovanni. Some people called him Jon, I preferred Giovanni, but it didn't matter what his name was. He was fit, and his Italian charm had me hooked. He was the best lover I'd ever had, and I'd had a fair few.

We both worked on the same cruise liner, but we hadn't had a night off together for months until now. I was meeting him in one of the ship's bars. I was excited.

I got dressed up in my best outfit and wore my hair straight. I looked good.

When I got to the bar, he was sitting at a table right near the front where the entertainment would be later. There was no mistaking his jet-black hair and beautiful olive skin. I got butterflies just looking at him.

I quickly realised he wasn't alone. He was with a girl I didn't recognise. She had long, blonde, wavy hair and wore a figure-hugging dress which was short enough to show off her long legs. She was very sexy. I felt instantly sick as I imagined a million different scenarios. We were supposed to be alone tonight. What was going on?

Was he seeing her behind my back, or was he seeing me behind her back? Had he slept with her? I briefly considered slipping away and going back to my cabin, but then he spotted me.

He waved me over. He appeared to be as happy to see me as I was him. The girl didn't move, but his enthusiasm made me feel slightly less concerned.

I walked over to them and he kissed me on the cheek.

'This is Rebecca,' he said nodding towards the girl and smiling. 'Rebecca, this is Ella.'

'Hi Rebecca,' I said politely. I wanted to ask who the fuck she was, but I played it cool.

'Don't worry,' whispered Giovanni as I sat down; 'she's not into men.'

Knowing that Rebecca wasn't after Giovanni made me feel better. I relaxed, and the three of us had a great night.

My new favourite drink was Bacardi and coke; I knocked back so many that I must have spent almost an entire month's wage.

The theme of the night was 'Swing Time with Fred and Ginger', and there was a Fred Astaire and Ginger Rogers tribute act. They were actually very good.

Giovanni said he was going out for a smoke. Weed was rife on the ship and he knew exactly where to get it.

I felt awkward being left alone with Rebecca, but it wasn't long before we were talking and laughing like old friends.

It made me think about Bess and Nessa. I missed them dearly, but I wrote to them loads and they to me. I was kept up to date with their lives, and I loved telling them about my life on the big cruise liners.

Rebecca suddenly leant across and put her hand on mine. 'You're stunning you know?'

This took me back to a night that I'd tried to forget. The night I had sex with my best friend, Bess. That night made her realise that she was a lesbian, but the memory often left me feeling sick because I wasn't. It had damaged our friendship for a short time, but fortunately, we'd managed to get through it.

Did Rebecca think I was a lesbian? Was I a lesbian? I had only ever been attracted to men, but then there had been that night with Bess. I was confused. The Bacardi wasn't helping.

Before I had time to respond, Giovanni was back.

'Ciao ladies,' he grinned, his beautiful white teeth shining brightly. He really was fit, and I was feeling drunk and in love.

He shouted the waiter over. It was one of our friends, Frej, and Giovanni persuaded him to get us a bottle of champagne.

'Come on. Let's take this back to my cabin,' he said.

Alarm bells started to ring in my head, but at the same

time, I felt extremely horny.

His cabin was bland as they all were, but he'd made it as homely as he could.

His work uniform hung on the rails of the cabin walls all clean and ironed. Big, fluffy, blue towels were folded up at the end of his bed. We cracked opened the Champagne which Frej had nicked for us.

'Rebecca thinks you're stunning,' Giovanni said, smiling. I could tell he was testing the water. I wanted him to like me, and so I went with it.

'I think Rebecca is stunning too,' I said flirtatiously, playing with my black bob.

I downed my glass of champagne. It gave me a little extra confidence.

'Does Rebecca want me to take my clothes off?' I asked. Giovanni was shocked but delighted. I was pleased I had shocked him; I didn't want him to think I was boring or prudish.

He didn't even look at Rebecca who sat giggling with her legs over the chair.

'Rebecca does,' he responded.

I slowly started to undo my shirt and laughed shyly as my tits popped out of my bra. I took off my bra, feeling turned on by the fact I had an audience. I twisted my nipples, pulling at them, as they both watched. I felt in control, almost powerful. I was wet, very wet.

I undid my pants and wriggled out of them, leaving me in just my black lace knickers.

I took a sip of the champagne straight from the bottle, licking the neck seductively as I did so.

Rebecca stood up and started to take her clothes off. She was also wearing black lace knickers. Her breasts were huge and complemented her tiny waist.

I leant over and brushed her nipples with my thumbs. 'Suck them,' she groaned.

I put my mouth over one of her nipples and flicked it softly with my tongue, then sucked it. She moaned with pleasure.

Giovanni was rubbing himself. I could see his hard cock bulging through his pants which looked as if they would burst.

Rebecca pushed me gently on the bed and started to kiss me hard on the lips. I kissed her back, loving the feeling of her soft mouth and warm, wet tongue.

I pushed her head down; I wanted that tongue somewhere else, I was aching for the feeling she was about to give me.

Giovanni had stripped off too.

'Touch her,' I told him.

He didn't have to be asked twice, and he put both his hands on her soft pale body and proceeded to rub her up and down, cupping her huge breasts from behind. She was moaning loudly as she licked me between my legs, her soft, warm tongue reaching places I hadn't known existed. I writhed on the bed pushing myself closer to her face. I wanted to wrap my legs tight around her neck.

I was in heaven but held on to my orgasm, so the moment didn't end.

I looked up and nearly jumped out of my skin.

A dead Richard Ellis was standing in Giovanni's cabin with a syringe sticking out of his neck. He was walking towards me like a zombie as Rebecca's tongue licked me up and down, my pussy throbbing hard. Giovanni was rocking to and fro, his cock firmly stuck in her arse.

Richard was getting nearer and nearer. He reached out to touch me, and I screamed.

****

I shot up in bed. The effort of trying to scream had woken me from my weird dream. I looked around and was relieved to see I was in my own cabin. I was sweaty and horny and shaking.

It wasn't the first time I'd had sexual dreams that had ended with him being there. It was like I couldn't escape him, Richard fucking Ellis, my biological father, my mum and sister's rapist.

I looked at my watch. It was almost time to get up anyway, so I rolled myself out of bed and into the shower.

'I need to call mum,' I thought to myself.

Chapter 2

Bess Holland

When I got my mum back, I vowed I would never leave my parents. It had been a difficult journey recovering from her abduction; even now, it still felt strange having her around. I wondered if she would ever fully recover from her ordeal.

She wasn't the mum I remembered, but in a way, she was better for it. She was stronger, more grounded and appreciated life so much more. She had moments where she'd go into her own little world, but she always bounced back. She rarely spoke about her ordeal; in the early days, she rarely spoke at all.

Mum had a wonderful way of dealing with things, and I admired her massively. She'd fallen back in love with my dad, and their bond was truly unbreakable. After years apart, it was clear that they'd never be apart again.

Dad was on a mission to be the best husband in the world. He still liked a drink but was drinking far less than before; I think it was just part of who he was.

I had come out as gay. My dad had let everyone know by accident. It wasn't a common thing on our estate, so I'd had to get used to the whispers. A couple of my hairdressing clients had stopped calling, but most weren't bothered; they probably didn't want to pay salon prices.

My best friends, Ella and Nessa, knew and had accepted it completely which was a huge relief. I thought back to my night of passion with Ella. I know she regretted it, but I didn't. I'd always secretly loved Ella, and it had been so confusing. That night helped me come to terms with being a lesbian and in a way, it helped me move on with my life. I was able to accept that Ella would never feel the same way towards me, but she would always be my first, and I treasured that.

Mum hadn't cared about me being gay either, and for that I was thankful. It made a difficult time much easier. It was hard being gay. I wasn't a stereotypical lesbian. I was little and blonde, very feminine and I loved pretty things. I found it difficult to settle in any relationship, but I didn't need one anyway; I was happy in my own world.

I still lived with my parents in the house I had grown up in. It hadn't always been a happy home, but along with the bad memories there were also a lot of good, and we were all happy there now.

Dad had extended our outhouse with the help of some of his builder mates. They made it into a small salon for me, with a backwash they had got hold of from another job they were working on. I had a smart little chair and a mirror with plugs for my hairdryer. It was perfect and all I needed.

I was having a cup of tea, waiting for my next client to arrive when the phone rang.

I guessed it was my next lady phoning to cancel and I was annoyed as I picked up the receiver and said 'Hello.'

It wasn't my next lady. It was the lady who had been like a mother to me while my own mother was missing. It was Christine Parker.

She told me that Ella was coming home and explained why. I'd thought things were getting back to normal, but now this.

Chapter 3

Nessa Brown

'Si? Are you awake yet?' I shouted up the stairs of our little house on the edge of the estate. We had bought it off the council after the birth of our first child Haydn, who I loved with all my heart. He was ten months old and had Si's black hair and my curls.

He hadn't been planned, but he was the best mistake we'd made to date.

Haydn gurgled happily in his high chair in the kitchen while I shouted up to his daddy to get out of bed. Si had been up all night with Haydn who was teething.

I looked out of the kitchen window as I waited for my partner to get up; I thought about my life so far.

I'd had a rocky start growing up in a house with a paedophile father, who had sexually abused my sister, Faya. We'd been put into care which was for the best, but it had been disruptive and upsetting for me as a child.

As soon as she was old enough, Faya had put her name down for a council flat and moved me in with her. It gave us both independence and taught us valuable lessons for the rest of our lives. We'd both grown into strong women who were making the most of the hand we'd been dealt.

Faya lived not far from us with her partner and little girl. It was as though we were finally allowed to be settled and happy.

I had my Si, my one and only true love. I'd loved him forever and I would always love him. He was my best friend and the best daddy to our little boy.

He had disappeared once out of my life and came back just at the right time.

I thought back to that night and the way Si had rescued me from my idiot of an ex, Tony. I'd been at Ella's leaving party and Tony had decided to attack me in the pub. As if from nowhere, my knight in shining armour came to my rescue and swooped me into his arms and into the night. It was like a movie.

I smiled as I remembered seeing his face for the first time after years of yearning for him.

We were very quickly in each other's arms making mad, passionate love. I smiled as I reminisced, then felt a wave of sadness too.

That was the same night that Josie Parker had been raped. I shuddered at the thought of that event and the ones that followed. We had plotted to kill Peter Lawrence, but he ended up killing Richard Ellis instead. Uncle Richard. That fucking pervert had a lot to answer for and Peter had known the whole story. I shook my head as I tried to forget it.

As Si came down the stairs wearing just a pair of boxer shorts and a t-shirt, the phone started to ring.

'I'll get it,' I shouted. 'You watch Haydn.'

Si smiled as he passed me, him going into the kitchen and me running to the phone in the living room.

'Hello,' I said into the receiver. All I could hear was breathing. I got a flashback to when this used to happen when Richard Ellis had been making our lives hell. I put the receiver down quickly and stood for a minute. It rang again.

'Hello?' I was more abrupt.

'What's up with you?' came Christine Parker's voice. It made me smile.

She told me Ella was coming home and then she explained why. I was shaking but promised to be there. They could count on me.

I put the phone down and listened to my son and partner playing in the kitchen. Si was pretending the spoon with food on it was a train and making 'choo choo' noises. It always made Haydn eat his food.

I was pacing up and down my living room. The wallpaper we had chosen was expensive; pale blue on the top with a flower border through the middle and dark blue on the bottom. My sofa was white with flowers to match the border. White wasn't the most practical choice when you had a ten-month-old baby, but I loved it.

I needed to get out. I was feeling anxious. I felt this way often, and it was no wonder after what we'd all been through.

I grabbed the car keys and shouted; 'I'm popping out love.'

'Ok love,' Si replied, 'take care.'

I drove to the other side of the estate. I didn't know where to go; I just needed some time out. I wondered whether I should call Bess or go to Chrissie's.

I was worked up. I knew that things were going to go a bit mad, but those girls were my life. Ella Parker and Bess Holland would kill for me; we'd kill for each other which we'd already proven.

Was it going to be like that again?

If Christine Parker was worried, then it was serious. The details she'd given me over the phone were playing on my mind.

I spotted Peter Lawrence. He looked like he'd come from the Parker house. That would have been strange a few years ago, but these days it wasn't unusual.

After Ella had gone to work on the ships, Christine Parker had sat Peter down and told him the truth about who he was. She had only found out herself the night that Richard had brutally murdered Helen Ellis.

That night, we had been so focused on getting revenge on Peter, that we had no idea what had been happening elsewhere.

Chrissie had known Richard was responsible for the attack on Josie. He had threatened her and Chris Parker years before.

She'd gone to confront him, ready to kill him for what he had done. When she arrived, she was shocked and confused to find Helen Ellis looking after a recently rescued Madge Holland.

Richard had returned to find the three women together. Three women who he'd terrorised for most of their adult lives. Three women embroiled in a web of lies, deceit and torture — a web that he had meticulously spun through intimidation, manipulation and sheer violence.

He'd tried to shoot Christine, but Helen had protected her, and in doing so, lost her life. It had devastated Madge and Christine who had desperately tried to save her.

They referred to Helen as the 'Dark Angel'. Chrissie said that's what she looked like and that she determined all our futures with her actions that night. It was so sad that she had never been free and then was killed by the man who kept her prisoner.

Richard had left after killing Helen. He came to the hotel where we were about to kill Peter. To this day, we had never worked out how he knew where we were or why he had gone there. Ultimately, it led to his death.

Madge had later explained to Chrissie that Peter was actually her husband's nephew, Kevin. Kevin's mum had been burnt to death in an 'accident' caused by a lit cigarette, and at the time, people assumed that Kevin had died too.

We would never know the truth about how baby Kevin, or Peter as he was now known, had escaped the blaze. We would also never know the circumstances around how he came to live with the Lawrence family. There was no doubt that Richard Ellis had orchestrated it somehow.

Peter had cried when Chrissie told him, but it helped him make sense of some things. Chris Parker, Ella's dad, had held him tightly and told him he was sorry, even though he had nothing to be sorry for.

Peter now had a family, and new bonds were formed. He had moved into Faya's old flat with his cousin, Henry Parker. It was the first time Peter had ever felt part of something.

I pulled up next to him.

'Do you want a lift Peter?' I asked. We'd never reverted to calling him Kevin.

He still had spit at the side of his mouth and an awkward gait. He was clumsy-looking, but his Irish eyes didn't look as dead anymore. I'm sure I saw a spark in them these days. Maybe it was hope.

Things could have been so different if, on that night, he'd

had taken another route with that syringe. For a moment, we all thought he was going to stick it in Si's neck. I was grateful that he hadn't.

'Alright Nessor?' He always put an 'or' sound at the end of my name. 'Yeah go on then. Thanks! I'm going back to the flat if that's alright?'

He got in the car. I remembered back to when I was actually scared of this man. Even as a boy he was scary. None of it was his fault; he was misunderstood, misguided and manipulated.

'Where've you been?' I asked him, and he explained that he'd been to see his Aunty Chrissie. It made me smile when he called her that. I expect it took her some getting used to, but he was part of their family now.

'Did you know Ella is coming home?' he said.

After what Chrissie had told me, I wasn't surprised that he knew what was going on.

'Yeah, I know. We'll have to wait and see what happens now, won't we?'

'Yeah,' he responded half listening to me.

'Let us out here, Nessor,' He said abruptly.

I pulled over, and he got out of the car without a word which was strange. I looked in my mirror and saw that he was talking to a bloke around the same age as us. I couldn't make out who he was, he didn't look familiar, which was unusual because we knew everyone around here. Peter looked awkward, but then he always did. I hesitated for a moment, but Peter walked off with him.

I drove off and thought no more of it; instead, I thought about getting home to my comfortable world. I wouldn't tell Si about my conversation with Chrissie, he wouldn't be happy.

Chapter 4

Ella Parker

I couldn't believe I was going home. Initially, I'd only agreed to one season on the cruise liners, but I'd now been away for three years.

When I applied, I had just wanted to get away from everything that was going on. My boyfriend Conny had been shot, and I'd slept with my best friend, Bess. Although our friendship recovered, it had been strained for about a year afterwards.

Then, my little sister had been raped; it was such a brutal attack. We didn't expect her to recover, but thankfully, she had. As a result, we'd set up a murder that would have been a terrible mistake.

I almost didn't take the job after my sister's ordeal and the events it triggered, but my family and friends persuaded me to stick to my plan.

I loved my first season, so when I got asked to stay on, I didn't hesitate. I couldn't refuse. Life was certainly different aboard the ships, and it had given me the escape I needed. I was now coming to the end of my third contract, and I'd loved it just as much as the years before.

The whole thing had given me an experience I'd have never gained if I'd have stayed on the estate. It had made me independent and taught me to make my own decisions. It had given me experiences of different cultures and people from all walks of life.

As I sat on the plane, approaching Manchester Airport, the captain announced that we were close to landing and that we had to buckle up.

I was nervous as I looked out of the plane window and almost wanted to ask the captain to turn around and take me back to the warmth of my cabin. I didn't know how I'd sleep without the ocean rocking me gently each night. I gulped; I missed it already.

I'd missed my family and I'd missed the girls, but I was worried it wouldn't be the same. So much had changed; what if I didn't fit in with their new lives? What if they didn't like the person I'd become?

It wasn't long before I found out. Mum and Dad were there to greet me at the airport. It was an emotional moment and I started crying as soon as I saw them. I ran towards mum who looked like she'd aged, and it made me feel sad.

'You alright love?' She beamed. 'God I've missed you.' She hugged me so tightly, I thought she'd never let go.

Dad rolled his eyes. 'Come here you pain in the arse,' he said. When mum let go, he gave me the tightest squeeze ever. I was crying hard now. I must have looked a right state.

We headed to the car park and dad paid for the ticket, moaning about the cost.

'Bloody rip off this place,' he mumbled.

I laughed. Not much had changed after all, I thought to myself.

It was a short journey back to my parent's house. I had forgotten how beautiful all the trees looked when the summer sun shone through all the pink blossoms. I felt excited to be home.

My brothers and sister were at our front door waving frantically as I got out of the car, and half the neighbours were outside watching my arrival. It was like I'd been let out of bloody prison or something, and the welcome overwhelmed me.

Mum made a great big Sunday dinner, even though it wasn't a Sunday. As my family chattered around the table, mum plonked a full loaf of buttered bread in the middle of all the plates. I thought it was almost rude for her to do that, but it was because I'd seen a different way of life now. Different but not better.

After dinner, there was a knock on the door and I felt apprehensive. I knew it would be them; I was both nervous and excited to see them.

My mum went to answer, and I prepared myself, taking deep breaths. Bess and Nessa walked into our living room and my nerves disappeared. We all embraced each other. Bess was crying, and Nessa was laughing.

'Where's Haydn?' I cried, 'I'm dying to meet him.'

Nessa explained that Haydn would be going to bed shortly, so she'd left him with Si. She still looked coy when she said his name. It was beautiful.

Soon we were laughing and chatting away, remembering the good times we'd had together.

'Remember when we went to Spain?' I laughed, 'we got off with those two Spanish lads, one of them looked like a rat.'

'Yeah, he was yours.' Nessa was laughing.

'What about how burnt we'd got because we put fuckin' carrot juice on us instead of proper sun cream.'

Mum came in and there was silence as she sat down with her cup of tea. I hadn't noticed that everyone else had disappeared out of the living room. They'd obviously been told to make themselves scarce.

'Right girls,' she said getting down to business. 'We need to decide what we are going to do?'

'We've made the mistake before of not taken things seriously; if I had done, then poor Josie wouldn't have gone through her ordeal.'

This was why I'd come home. I had been in two minds about signing another contract and then I'd spoken to my mum. She'd said a few things that concerned me, and I decided I needed to come back and be here for the people who meant the most to me. I could always go back to the ships, but I'd never forgive myself if I wasn't there and something happened to one of my family or my girls.

'We got rid of Richard Ellis thinking that would be that, but his son Richard fuckin' junior is wanting some sort of penance for the death of his parents,' mum continued.

She looked sad and I know she was thinking of Helen Ellis who had saved her life. She had probably saved Madge's life too. We owed a lot to that woman, our 'Dark Angel'.

'Peter was here the other day,' she said, 'and he told me

that young Richard seems to know exactly what happened to his father. I don't know if he knows anything for sure or if he's just guessing, but he doesn't believe for a minute that his dad was with prostitutes in that seedy hotel.'

I felt sick. Nobody could ever find out what happened; we could all go to prison.

As far as the police were concerned, Richard had been killed by prostitutes. I doubt they believed that, but it was what had gone in the reports. He had been manipulating and blackmailing most of his colleagues in the police force, so they were probably concerned that one of their own had killed him. This had worked in our favour as they had barely investigated his death.

We had covered our tracks as best we could, but if they'd done more digging, they might easily have got to the truth. Luckily, they didn't care very much, especially when it came to light that he'd shot his wife and had kept a woman locked up as a prisoner for over a decade. He was an embarrassment, so they wanted the whole thing put to rest quickly and quietly.

I shook my head and jumped up out my seat. I was pissed off.

'Are you sure Peter isn't just making it up? I mean he's not right in the head, is he? I can't believe this; I feel sick. I can just see us all locked up for fuck sake.'

'Calm down Ella love,' said mum. 'Where's jumping up and down going to get us?'

Ness laughed. 'You're such a drama queen,' she said. 'Let's hear the rest of the story first. At least then we can organise visiting orders for our friends and family.'

'It's not funny Ness. That could happen,' I said, not impressed with her jokes.

'Well, I think that's why your mum has us here now so that we can stop that from happening,' said Bess, always so sensible.

'Exactly Bess,' mum said, 'exactly.'

'And how do we stop that from happening?' I said.

I was serious. If this man knew the truth, he would

always know the truth, and we would spend the rest of our lives worrying about it. We couldn't live under that cloud; the cloud was heavy enough without this.

'I don't know,' mum said, 'but he's getting near and he's started to 'accidentally' bump into Peter. He knows Peter's not a full shilling so he's making threats about what he's going to do to him. It's like history repeating itself, and I don't like it.'

'So, if he knows it's Peter who killed him,' I said, 'why are we worried?'

'Because, Ella Parker, I've brought you up to be loyal. Peter might have killed him, but you were there too, so you're not so innocent yourself lady.'

Mum's nostrils had started to flare like they did when she was fuming.

'That man made a lot of lives a misery; he was vile to the bone. He raped me, he raped your sister, he held Bess's mum prisoner and murdered the woman who saved my life. He deserved to die, and we owe it to Peter to protect him. Do you know it was because of me, his mother was killed? That should have been me in there, not her. And he's family. If you've not got the message by now young lady, then you're not who I thought you were.'

We sat in silence, shocked by mum's outburst. I felt ashamed for even considering letting Peter take the fall by himself.

Thankfully, a banging on the front door broke the atmosphere. Dad came downstairs and opened it.

'Jesus Christ! What happened son?'

He helped Peter through to the living room and sat him down. He'd been battered black and blue; I felt sick for him.

He really didn't deserve this; he had been robbed of his mother as a tiny boy, then bullied and battered all his life. We'd even given him a hard time and tried to kill him. It was no wonder he was the way he was; he'd had all his senses knocked out of him. And here he was with a busted lip and swollen eye, and the poor lad wouldn't hurt a fly.

I looked over at mum with tears in my eyes.

'You're absolutely right. We owe it to him and we need to stick together. And we will.'

'Yeah we will,' Nessa and Beth said at the same time, and we turned our attention to Peter.

'You ok, Peter?' I asked him.

He looked up slowly. He was clearly in a lot of pain.

'I'm ok, but David's not,' he said, and with that he passed out.

Chapter 5

Bess Holland

Peter was taken to casualty at the local hospital where he was checked over, given painkillers and told to rest. He needed a couple of stitches in his busted lip. Poor lad; he'd had such a shit time, it was hard to believe.

He was confused when he came round. He was always confused, but you could tell he'd had a bump to the head.

Once we knew he was ok, me, Ella and Nessa decided to go out. It was the first time in years we'd been together, and we needed a night to celebrate. Chrissie wasn't happy when we told her, but we reassured her that we'd be careful.

Ella asked her dad for a tenner and I roared with laughter. She didn't change, and I realised how much I had missed her.

We drove to Nessa's so she could grab some clothes and makeup. Ella said a quick hello to Si and peeked in on baby Haydn.

'He's beautiful' she cried, 'he looks just like you Ness.'

Once they'd both sorted themselves out with what they needed, we went to mine to get ready. We started in my salon where I did their hair for them. Ella had brought a bottle of champagne that she'd nicked off the ships.

It felt just like the old days except my mum was here with us as we chatted away. She had never seen the three of us together like this. She loved it and was enjoying the banter. Even though the girls had been coming here since they were six years old, they didn't know my mum, so they were being especially respectful.

It didn't stop them telling her stories about us growing up, and she sat in awe and really listened, smiling the whole time.

I thought about all the years she'd missed, me thinking she had abandoned me.

Ella was an excellent storyteller; she was always adding

bits in and exaggerating events.

Mum was in tears of laughter. It made me sad to think that I'd been having so much fun while she'd been locked up wondering if she'd ever see me again.

'My god; you girls are like sisters. I could never imagine a closeness like this,' said mum.

I looked at Ella and hoped and prayed she wouldn't mention just how close we had gotten; she was giddy, and I wouldn't have put it past her.

But she didn't.

Our laughter was broken by the shout of my dad.

'You here Bess?'

He'd been for his usual pint but was home early, and he wasn't falling through the door pissed like he used to.

Ella ran to greet him, throwing her arms around his big shoulders.

'Alright kid?' He was pleased to see her. 'We've bloody missed you. Missed your big gob,' he joked, and everybody started laughing.

I don't think I have felt happier than I did at that moment with both my girls and both my parents together. It was like my dreams had come true.

We finished getting ready up in my bedroom and compared outfits. Ella had gone all browns and mustards with a white, fake-leather mac.

Nessa had a black two-piece on, black leggings with a boot flare, and a matching fitted top that showed off her huge breasts and shapely figure.

I settled for a silk purple two-piece, a flared skirt matched with what looked like a pyjama top.

'We still look the bollocks,' Ella laughed, staring at herself in the huge mirror on my bedroom wall.

'I look fuckin' huge,' complained Nessa.

'You've just had a baby,' me and Ella said at once.

'I look like that girl who turns into a blueberry in Charlie and the Chocolate Factory,' I said.

They both looked me up and down dead serious for a minute before bursting out laughing. They both started singing 'Oompa Loompa diddly doo' at the top of their voices.

When we finally composed ourselves again and were sorting out the finishing touches, Ella got serious.

'What did Peter mean when he said I'm ok, but David's not? That's what he said isn't it? What did he mean? Who's David?'

'God; I forgot about that,' Nessa said, putting a layer of lipstick on top of the thirty layers she'd already put on.

'I'm not sure,' I said, 'but I think Richard Ellis had a son called David. Maybe it's Richard Junior's brother?'

An almighty crash came from outside my bedroom door. I quickly opened it and found mum staring at a tray and three glasses of wine that were on the floor. She was visibly shaking and devastated that she'd dropped everything.

Ella grabbed hold of her; 'Are you ok? Come and sit on the bed for a minute.'

Nessa started to clean up the mess on the landing, running downstairs for a dustpan and brush.

'I'm sorry girls,' said mum. 'I wasn't listening, I just wanted to bring you some drinks. Then I heard his name just as I got to the door and it knocked me for six. Why were you talking about that family? And what is wrong with David?'

'Just Peter talking nonsense again mum, nothing to worry about.' I wasn't convincing in my lie, but I didn't want to worry her.

She went on to tell us about David. He'd found her when she was locked up, and they'd talked right through the night. He'd been such a comfort for her and had promised to come back for her. She told us how she waited for him to come back for days and later found out that young Richard had attacked him and put him in intensive care.

'So he sent his mother,' she said. 'If it hadn't been for David and his mum, I'd never have got out. There's an older brother too, called Robert. He's the double of his mum. He's a policeman, but he's nothing like his father.'

We listened intently, and I felt awful for her. It must have been terrible suddenly hearing his name and being reminded of her ordeal.

I was also worried because this young Richard Ellis was clearly cut from the same cloth as his father. Maybe his threats to Peter were real.

'Anyway girls,' she said cheerfully, 'you get yourselves out. You didn't get all dressed up to sit here with me.'

'Are you sure you're ok?' I asked.

'Of course, darling.' She smiled. 'I wouldn't have it any other way. Take your dad out for one too, just make sure he's not out all night.'

'He's only just come in,' said Nessa laughing

'Well, believe me,' mum said, 'he won't mind.'

I wanted to stay with mum a bit longer, but she was having none of it.

'Go on bugger off out,' she said, smiling broadly. 'I'm really ok.'

I reminded myself that if she was strong enough to survive what she had alone, she'd be ok without me for a couple of hours.

Chapter 6

Nessa Brown

I felt nervous about the three of us going to The Lion together, especially considering what we'd just been talking about. It had been a long time since that horrific night, but not long enough to be over it completely.

'You ok Ness?'

Bess could always read my emotions.

'Yeah, fine. It's just Ella coming home has brought a lot of stuff back up. I mean, I'm glad she's back, of course I am, but It's like all that stuff that happened went away with her, and now it's back. It just makes me nervous. The thought that this young Richard knows what happened scares the shit out of me. Do you get me?'

'Yeah I get you,' Bess was sincere. 'It'll be ok, you know. We can get through anything together.'

I wasn't so sure, but I wanted to forget about it and enjoy the night out with my best friends. I didn't get out often since having baby Haydn; it was nice to have a break.

The atmosphere was buzzing in 'The Lion'. The news that Ella was home had hit the estate and there were people in there that we'd not seen for years.

I was gobsmacked to see Skidder Barker in there. She was draped all over a good-looking bloke who looked really familiar.

We had grown up with Skidder. She'd bullied me in my early school years; Nessa the tramp she used to call me. I recalled a particular incident that probably scarred her more than it did me.

She tripped me up in the playground and sat on top of me to spit in my face. The memories came flooding back and I felt a bit sickly. My sister had pulled her off me and she went flying, exposing her shit-stained knickers to half the school. That's what earnt her the name Skidder, which everyone still called her to this day.

I didn't want to look at her, but she'd spotted me.

'Alright Vanessa?' she sneered.

I didn't like her using my full name.

I nodded my head and looked again at the man she was with. His eyes sparkled, but there was something not quite right about them. It was almost as though the sparkle was something sinister. And he looked so familiar.

'Where's your baby tonight? It's Hadyn isn't it?' she asked.

'He's with his dad,' I said. Why the fuck was she asking about my son?

'Nice,' she said. 'We've got some babysitting of our own to do.' She grinned, and her bloke smiled in a way that unnerved me. 'See you very soon Vanessa,' she said, and they left.

My stomach did a somersault. Something didn't feel right. Why was she so interested in me? Who was that creepy bloke she was with? And why would I see her 'very soon'?

I tried to convince myself I was being paranoid. It was just the excitement of Ella being back, and the trouble between Peter and the Ellis boy.

I looked over at Ella and smiled. She was hugging Lizzie and George. Lizzie was gushing loudly; 'We've missed you. It's not been the same without you.'

Ella was revelling in the attention as usual, hugging them back and enjoying the free drinks that were being bought for her. She couldn't just settle for half a lager when other people were paying; she'd get the most expensive drink she could. Tonight, it was Pernod and blackcurrant, and she had nearly a table full of them already.

Bess's dad was well-known and well-respected in here and always got the best table with the rest of the local in-crowd.

Bess and I walked over to join them.

'I told that Skidder Barker and her fella to fuck off,' Jon told us. 'Hanging about without buying a drink; probably just here to stir up trouble.'

I smiled and wondered why I still felt scared of Skidder fuckin' Barker. She probably just wanted to see what was going on. She was a nosey cow and always had been.

The next few hours flew by. We were having a great time, laughing, taking the piss out of each other, catching up and reminiscing. I had missed it.

'You having a good time?' I asked Ella. I could tell she was pretty drunk by now.

'It's mad,' she said, 'I've been all over the world now and met so many people, but there really is no place like home.'

I was glad she was happy to be back. It was good to see her again.

One of Jon's mates, Macca, came in the pub and shouted something. It immediately quietened down, everyone trying to hear what he was saying.

'It's fucking kicking off up at the next block. Some geezer is hanging out of one of the flat windows with a little kid. Looks like he's either going to jump or throw the kid off. He's in the block opposite the shops in that flat that's been empty for months, the one Dave Lee's ex lived in before she shacked up with his brother. There's a right crowd.'

'Who is it Macca?' Jon Holland shouted across.

'Don't know him Jon, but he was with that Skidder Barker earlier; someone said they heard her call him Richard. The blokes a nutter; Skidder's fucked off.'

It suddenly dawned on me why I recognised the man Skidder had been with. He was the bloke Peter had been talking to when I dropped him off the other day.

I looked across at Ella and Bess and widened my eyes at them. We headed outside.

'Do any of you know what young Richard Ellis looks like?' I asked them both.

They both shook their head.

'I saw a lad with Peter the other day. I didn't know who he was, but it was the same bloke that was in here tonight with Skidder. Macca just said the bloke hanging out the

167

window was with Skidder and that someone had called him Richard. It can't be a coincidence. How many Richard's would Peter know and why would a good-looking bloke like that be hanging around with Skidder?'

'Come on,' said Bess, 'let's see what's going on.'

A crowd of people had come outside and were heading towards the flats Macca had mentioned. Curiosity had clearly got the better of them, and they were off to see what was happening.

We followed the crowd which was getting animated. It was almost like one big family going for an evening walk; it felt exciting.

I looked at the girls who were on either side of me, and I couldn't believe that the three of us were marching together again. We were like soldiers in a war with a mission in all our minds.

It took about ten minutes to get there, and there was quite a crowd. The flats were on big grass verges with flagged pavements leading up to them. Macca had been right; there was some idiot sat on a window ledge with a child who looked to be sleeping on his lap. I thought of my baby boy at home fast asleep and wondered where that child's mum was and why she'd left it with Richard Ellis.

'Someone's been up to see if they can smash the door down,' I heard a woman say. 'But he's had a security door fitted; the type the old bill can't kick down. The ones the druggies have so they can't get raided.'

It was dark; the orange street lights barely lit up the streets, never mind the face of a three-storey block of flats.

All of a sudden, the baby cried out. My breasts immediately started tingling like they did when Haydn cried. A horrible feeling ran over my body like a film of sweat.

I had such an intense feeling. That was my baby up there, I knew it. That's why Skidder was asking about Haydn and that's what she meant by babysitting.'

My whole body went hot, and my bowels nearly opened there and then. I looked at the crowd who were becoming a blur to me; everything had started moving in slow motion. It was my baby. Where was Si? I looked around helplessly and grabbed the girls.

'It's Haydn. That's Haydn up there with him. I know it's him; I know his cry. He's going to kill my baby.'

Chapter 7

Madge Holland

The girls and Jon left. I hadn't been this unsettled in years, and I paced the house feeling like a caged animal. They'd said David was in trouble and that had worried me. He had saved me and lost his mother through doing so.

Although he was a man, he wasn't much older than my own child. The fact that I'd had sex with him had long been forgotten. This wasn't what it was about. I owed it to him and Helen to make sure he was ok.

I knew exactly who would help me.

I ran into the living room and looked through the little red diary next to the phone. It was full of hand-written names and telephone numbers all in alphabetical order.

I found her under 'C' and dialled her number.

'Hello?'

'Chrissie. it's Madge.'

'What's up?'

I got straight to the point. There wasn't much time.

'The girls said that Peter told them that David wasn't ok.'

'He did.'

'He must have been talking about David Ellis. We need to help him Christine.'

She went silent for what seemed like an age, then finally said; 'I'll pick you up in ten minutes.'

I couldn't believe that after all I'd been through, I was once again getting involved in something I should steer clear of. But I knew that Helen would want someone to check that David was ok. I owed her. I owed them both.

Christine, true to her word, beeped her horn outside my door ten minutes later.

'Thanks for coming,' I said gratefully as I got into the car. I was nervous; I didn't often leave the house.

'We need to find out what Peter meant when he said

David wasn't ok,' I said.

'I didn't think anything of it at the time,' said Christine. 'I was so concerned about the fact Peter was so badly injured, I didn't pay much attention to what he was saying.'

We drove to the flat that Peter shared with Christine's son and knocked on the door.

Peter answered. His face looked a mess and I felt sorry for him. All his life he'd been battered and beaten and pushed around. Poor boy.

'What's up?' He looked surprised to see us both.

'We need to speak to you.' Christine said, letting herself in. I wasn't far behind her.

'Come in,' he said. I didn't know if he was being sarcastic or genuine. I'm not sure he had it in him to be sarcastic, so it was probably the latter.

I looked around and was surprised at how homely it looked. There was a definite boy-smell to it, but all in all, it was a lovely flat. There was a 'Stone Roses' poster on one wall and a 'Reservoir Dogs' one, on the other.

Christine and I stood awkwardly.

'Peter, we need to know what you meant when you said that David wasn't ok.' Christine was firm but gentle with him.

He looked as though he was thinking hard about something. Then it was as though he'd had an epiphany.

'Oh shit! I forgot.' He grabbed his face. He looked genuinely devastated. 'He's where you were Madge. Richard told me. He told me he had his brother all locked up there, in the place where you were.'

We all ran out of the flat and jumped into Christine's car.

As we drove past the airport and down towards Wilmslow, I thought about the last time I'd driven here. I thought about all the years I was incarcerated at the hands of that monster. I thought about the night with David and how beautiful it had been. I thought about my husband who I loved with all my heart and soul and my beautiful daughter who I adored. And I thought about Helen – the dark angel who had died without ever knowing true happiness. I swallowed my tears; I had to get to David.

The cobbled path made me feel sick as Christine drove along it as carefully as she could.

As we approached the big iron gates of the huge house, I wasn't sure how we were even going to get in. The gas lamp was lit; I wondered how it kept going after all these years and again thought of Helen and wondered how she had kept going.

'We need to get to the little house. It's in the woods,' Peter said, looking right at me as though I had the answer. It was then I noticed that the big iron gates were open ever so slightly.

The three of us jumped out of the car, and in calm silence, we pushed open the iron gates enough to allow Chrissie's car to fit through.

We drove around the back of the house and across the field which led to the thick woods. My mind took me back to when I'd had to walk across here from my prison to Helen's beautiful home. I shuddered.

'I think it's around the back of here,' said Peter, trying to remember where the house was hidden.

We approached a definite opening which I recognised.

'Go down there if you can Chrissie,' I said and pointed to the opening.

She switched her headlights to full beam and drove down a dirt path straight to the derelict house. I wanted to throw up. I never thought I'd see this place again, nor had I ever wanted to.

It was eerie in the darkness of the night. We got out of the car, and Chrissie and I instinctively held on to Peter's hand. He was another victim and he shouldn't even be here with us tonight.

We got to the door and turned the handle; it opened. The silence was overwhelming, but I knew David was here somewhere, and I wouldn't give up. He hadn't given up on me.

The roof was missing on part of the house, and wild ivy grew from the top of it. Chrissie had left the engine running on the car and the headlights were shining in. We saw a door at the end of a very dark corridor.

It was the room. It was my room. I felt sick.

Chrissie tried the door; it was locked.

'David. David' are you in there?' she shouted. There was no answer.

We searched around the other rooms, jumping as cobwebs touched our faces. We gripped each other's hands tightly, hoping that we weren't too late.

'He's not here. You must have it wrong,' Chrissie said. She wanted to get out of here as much as me and Peter did. We left the house. An owl hooted, and again we all jumped.

'For fuck sake,' cried Chrissie. 'Let's get the fuck out of here.'

'Wait!' I said.

I couldn't leave without checking 'my room'.

'We need to kick that door down. I just know he's in there.'

Christine Parker looked at me as though I'd gone mad. Perhaps I had, but I couldn't go without checking behind that door.

Once again, we entered the dark house feeling no braver than we had thirty seconds ago.

The door was old and battered. The three of us lunged at it until we finally fell through it into a heap on the floor.

'Jesus!' I cried.

Chrissie saw him too.

'My god! Untie him. Peter go to the back of my car and look in the boot for any scissors or anything and see if there are clothes or blankets in there. Bring what you can.'

Peter ran to the car while we made a start.

David had been tied up. He was naked and wrapped in thick masking tape which held his hands and feet together and covered his mouth.

His brother had left him for dead. No one would have ever found him here.

Chrissie and I tried to get the tape off, but it was hard in the dark. We were hurting him by tugging roughly at the tape. We cleared the tape from his face so he could talk. As he spoke, I could tell how weak he was.

'How long have you been here?' I asked him, remembering that he once asked me the same question.

'A few days,' he said.

Peter ran back in with everything useful he'd found in Chrissie's boot which was a bread knife, a blanket and her husband's coat.

'Well done Peter,' Chrissie praised him.

'Come on lad,' she said to David, 'let's get this shit off you.'

'We need to get to the estate,' he said as we cut away at the tape with a blunt bread knife. 'He's got plans and they don't sound good. He's convinced you murdered my father.'

'He sounds as mad as your father,' said Chrissie, 'let's get out of here.'

Wearing a blanket around his bottom half and Chris Parker's coat on the top half, David staggered to the car.

'I need to get something from the house,' said David.

He went in and returned minutes later, properly dressed and dangling a set of keys.

'He's got himself a hideaway, but I know exactly where it is, and I know where he hides the spare keys.'

'Let's go,' I said. I was glad to see the back of that house, and I vowed never to come here again.

As we approached the estate, we noticed a crowd gathered outside a block of flats.

'I knew it,' David said. 'This will be something to do with him.'

I saw Bess in the crowd with Ella and Nessa. Chrissie spotted them too. We looked up to see what they were staring at.

Young Richard Ellis sat on a window ledge holding a small child.

Chapter 8

Nessa Brown

I couldn't see my baby's face but I recognised the baby grow he had on. I could sense him, and his cry was sending me into turmoil.

Hot bile bubbled in the back of my throat. I ran to the front of the crowd and shouted up to Richard.

'Please, Richard,' I begged. 'He's just a baby, don't do this.'

'You killed my dad,' he called back to me in a calm voice.

I couldn't see Ella or Bess, but I saw Madge and Chrissie coming toward me. I was confused. I started to hyperventilate, and Madge rubbed my back.

Blue lights were flashing around me.

Policemen were arriving in black vests and armed with guns. Everything was deathly silent. Everything felt like it was happening in slow motion.

Chapter 9

Ella Parker

Nessa ran to the front of the crowd; she was calling up to that maniac, begging him not to hurt Haydn.

I spotted Peter heading towards the flat.

'What's Peter doing here?' I whispered to Bess.

He beckoned us over and put his finger on his lips. We ran over to him.

Peter whispered 'I've got the keys to the flat. We need to get in and stop him.'

'We need to be careful Peter,' I said, 'that's Nessa's baby he's holding.'

'Shit!' Peter said.

I was shaking from head to toe as the adrenalin pumped hard through my body. I was going in with Peter, no matter what happened and so was Bess.

We walked up three flights of stairs which stunk of piss. Peter gave Bess the keys so that she could open the door, allowing us to gain entry. She was cool as anything as she gently unlocked the heavy steel door. We very slowly pushed it open, hoping and praying we wouldn't make a noise.

We could hear him calling down to the crowd. Peter lunged forward in an attempt to grab baby Haydn. The next few seconds were crucial.

Young Richard had a knife. He slashed Peter across the chest, but he wasn't quick enough. Peter had snatched baby Haydn from his arms which sent him off balance. I held tightly to Bess as we watched Richard Ellis fall from the ledge.

Chapter 10

Nessa Brown

I was barely breathing as I watched a scramble on the ledge and then a body falling to the ground. I heard a thud and gasps from the crowd behind me.

I ran towards him as I pushed at people who seemed to want to block my way. Where was my baby?

A tall policeman beat me to the body. We were both looking for Haydn. Where the fuck was he?

I could hear the chaos of the crowd. Where were the girls? Where was Haydn? I could hear the sirens of an ambulance. I could hear people crying with relief and then I heard my baby crying. And I saw them with my boy in their arms.

I ran towards them and collapsed in their arms crying. I held on to my son so tightly while Ella and Bess held on to me.

A paramedic was treating the knife wound on Peter's chest. He needed stitches, but luckily it wasn't deep enough to do any real damage. Peter Lawrence had more lives than a fucking cat.

'What happened?' I asked the tall policeman. His amber eyes were the most beautiful, kindest eyes I'd ever seen.

'We don't know the full story,' he told me, 'but he apparently hooked up with a lady called Linda Barker, and they concocted a plan to kidnap your son. We'll let you know more when we have the details. We've got Linda Barker in custody.'

Linda was Skidder's real name. I knew she was a bitch, but I never thought she would be capable of doing this.

'Where's my boyfriend, Simon Bailey?' I was almost too scared to ask.

'He's ok. The police are going to bring him up later. He's had to be checked out at the hospital.'

I gasped. Poor Si. I started crying again.

I looked over to young Richard Ellis who was being covered up. When I looked back at the policeman, he had tears in his eye.

'He was my brother,' he said. 'I'm Robert Ellis.'

As he introduced himself, Madge and Chrissie came towards us with another man.

'That's my other brother, David,' Robert explained.

Chapter 11

Christine Parker

We stood together in silence; me and Madge, Nessa Ella and Bess, and the two Ellis brothers. Peter came over and joined us.

We were all part of a web that had been spun by the callous Richard Ellis. It was a web of destruction that spanned over two generations and changed the lives of so many people.

But in that web, there had always been hope. Hope for everyone who had been snared in it.

It was that hope that made us who we all were today.

We'd all survived, and we were finally free of his tangled web. All except one.

The Dark Angel.

Welcome Theo
Goodbye my beautiful hero

Lightning Source UK Ltd.
Milton Keynes UK
UKHW040616230819
348430UK00003B/1053/P